S0-BRK-074

UNIVERSITY LIBRARY

ST.
JOSEPH'S
UNIVERSITY
1851

Phil .. Pa.

FOR REFERENCE

Do Not Remove From Library

THEODORE PARKER

GARLAND REFERENCE LIBRARY
OF THE HUMANITIES
(VOL. 307)

THEODORE PARKER
A Descriptive Bibliography

Joel Myerson

ST. JOSEPH'S UNIVERSITY   **REF**

BX9869.P3M96
Theodore Parker, a descriptive bibliogra

3 9353 00104 6679

ST.
JOSEPH'S
UNIVERSITY
1851
Phil . . a.

UNIVERSITY LIBRARY

BX
9869
.P3
M96

GARLAND PUBLISHING, INC. · NEW YORK & LONDON
1981

194424

©1981 Joel Myerson
All rights reserved

Library of Congress Cataloging in Publication Data

Myerson, Joel.
   Theodore Parker, a descriptive bibliography.

   (Garland reference library of the humanities ;
v. 307)
   Includes index.
    1. Parker, Theodore, 1810–1860—Bibliography.
I. Title. II. Series.
Z8660.64.M96 [BX9869.P3]   016.288′092′4   81-43354
ISBN 0-8240-9279-1   AACR2

Printed on acid-free, 250-year-life paper
Manufactured in the United States of America

CONTENTS

v

INTRODUCTION

This descriptive bibliography of the works of Theodore Parker is limited to writings by Parker. Writings about Parker are not listed, except in cases where they include something by him published for the first time.

Format

Section A lists chronologically all books, pamphlets, and broadsides wholly by Parker, including all printings of all editions in English through 1980.

The numbering system for Section A indicates the edition and printing for each entry. Thus for *Critical and Miscellaneous Writings, A 6.3.d* indicates that this is the sixth title published by Parker (*A 6*), and that the entry describes the third edition (*3*), fourth printing (*d*). Issues are indicated by inferior numbers—thus *A 29.2.a₂* is the second issue of the first printing of the second edition of *Speeches, Addresses, and Occasional Sermons.* No examples of states have been found in Parker's works.

Each entry begins with a quasi-facsimile transcription of the title page, then gives pagination information and a collation of the gatherings. A description of the contents is supplemented in the notes, when needed, by a printing history of the volume's contents, giving each item's first appearance in print. Information on typography and paper includes the dimensions of the page and of the printed text, type of paper, number of lines per page, and running heads. Thus 5" X 3" indicates the height and width of the page or the area containing the text on a page; 5" (4½") X 3" indicates the height (first from the top of the running head to the bottom of the last line of text, and second from the top of the first line of text to the bottom of the last line of text) and width of the printed area. The description does not include leaf thickness or sheet bulk because there is no case for Parker in which these measurements are required to differentiate printings. All paper is white unless otherwise indicated. Binding information includes cloth types, descriptions of stampings, and notes on flyleaves, endpapers, page trimming, and page-edge gilding or staining. All wrappers are paper unless otherwise indicated. No dust jackets have been located for Section A entries. Information on printing and publication is drawn from Parker's published letters and journals, the records of Roberts Brothers, and copyright information (both the published and manuscript records of the Copyright Office). Locations are provided to identify the libraries holding copies of each title described. Notes deal with information not discussed elsewhere in the entry.

Section B lists chronologically all collected editions of Parker's writings in English.

Section C lists chronologically all miscellaneous collections of and selections from Parker's writings in English through 1973, the date of the last located item. Binding is assumed to be cloth or boards unless otherwise indicated. Locations are given for the copies examined.

Section D lists chronologically all books edited by Parker. Binding is assumed to be cloth or boards unless otherwise indicated. Locations are given for the copies examined.

Section E lists chronologically miscellaneous material not by Parker but often attributed to him, as well as numerous "spirit messages" from Parker to various mediums.

Terms and Methods

Edition. All copies of a book printed from a single setting of type—including all reprintings from standing type, from plates, or by photo-offset processes.

Printing. All copies of a book printed at one time (without removing the type or plates from the press).

State. States occur only within single printings and are created by an alteration not affecting the conditions of publication or sale to *some* copies of a given printing (by stop-press correction or cancellation of leaves). There must be two or more states. No states have been discovered in Parker's works.

Issue. Issues occur only within single printings and are created by an alteration affecting the conditions of publication to *some* copies of a given printing (usually a title leaf alteration). There cannot be a first issue without a second.

Edition, printing, state, and *issue* have here been restricted to the sheets of a book.[1]

Publishers' advertisements have been described but the reader should be aware that they generally exist in three forms. First, they may be integral with the first or last gatherings of a book. In such cases, variants between the advertisements can be used to determine the printing history of the book, since the advertisements were printed in the same press run as the rest of the work. Second, in a few cases, advertisements may be imprinted on the endpapers of a book. While useful in determining when a copy may have been bound, these advertisements do not bear on a book's printing history. Likewise, the third form, inserted catalogues of publishers' advertisements, may indicate only binding and not publication histories. It can be stated unequivocally that the date on the inserted advertisements in a book has no bearing on the priority of a printing.

For binding-cloth designations I have used the method proposed by G. Thomas Tanselle;[2] most of these cloth grains are illustrated in Jacob Blanck, *Bibliography of American Literature* (New Haven: Yale University Press, 1955–).

Color specifications are based on the *ISCC–NBS Color Name Charts Illustrated with Centroid Colors* (National Bureau of Standards). Centroid numbers have not been assigned; instead, the general color designations have been used.[3]

The spines of bindings have been printed horizontally unless otherwise indicated. The reader is to assume that vertically printed spines read from top to bottom unless otherwise indicated.

In the descriptions of the title pages and bindings, the color of the lettering is always black unless otherwise indicated.

Pagination for reprintings of Section A entries and for entries in Sections B through E indicates the number of the last printed page in the book, exclusive of publishers' advertisements.

I have made no attempt to comprehensively list Parker's

contributions to newspapers, magazines, and books.[4] Because so many of Parker's works in these media were unsigned, such a list will have to wait for the completion of the editions of Parker's letters and journals being prepared by, respectively, Gary L. Collison and Carol Johnston.

Copyright on Parker's works prior to 1871 was registered with the clerk of the District Court of Massachusetts in two stages: first, the book's title was given and entered into the copyright books, then a copy of the published work was deposited. Both these dates are given when available.

This bibliography is based upon evidence gathered from my personal inspection and collation of multiple copies of Parker's works. For first English and American editions, only libraries holding copies that are bibliographically intact (not rebound or repaired) are listed. Exceptions are rebound copies representing the only located example of the work or containing nonbibliographical information, such as dated owners' inscriptions, which are mentioned in notes. The symbols used for American libraries are those employed by the National Union Catalog; those for British libraries are the same as those listed in the *British Union-Catalogue of Periodicals*, which are here preceded by *B*. The following is an additional symbol:

JM   Collection of Joel Myerson

This bibliography is not an attempt to indicate the scarcity of Parker's works and should not be taken as such. If there is only one location given, it means that of all the libraries I visited or corresponded with, only one had or reported having a copy with all the examined points intact; it does not mean that there is only one copy of that work in existence. For recent editions I have not listed as many locations as for earlier ones, where I have tried to be as comprehensive as possible.

A bibliography is more than just a listing of books; it is also a detailed study of an author's literary career. Readers of this book will find information on Parker's literary reputation, as measured by sales of his books; the popularity of Parker's writings in England, as seen in the numerous editions and reprintings of his works abroad; and the textual history of Parker's works.

A bibliography is outdated the day it goes to the printer. Addenda and corrigenda are earnestly solicited.

This bibliography is part of my ongoing study of American Transcendentalism. In compiling it I have incurred many debts of gratitude. Unhappily, I can only thank in a general way the many librarians who answered my questions about copies of Parker's works at their institutions. I wish to express my appreciation to the following libraries and their staffs for help in using their collections: American Antiquarian Society, Andover-Harvard Theological School Library, Boston Athenæum, Boston Public Library, The British Library, Brown University Library, Cambridge University Library, Concord Free Public Library, Duke University Library, Harvard University Libraries (Houghton and Widener), Indiana University Library, Library of Congress, Little, Brown and Company, Massachusetts Historical Society, National Library of Scotland, New York Public Library, Oxford University Library (Bodleian Library), Princeton University Library, Stanford University Library, University of North Carolina Library, University of Texas Library, University of Virginia Library, and Yale University Library. The University of South Carolina has also been useful, and Harriet Oglesby has been both patient and skillful in obtaining books for me on loan.

Many people have helped in this project and I would especially like to thank the following: Barbara Bergeron, Gary L. Collison, Virginia Creeden, Carol Johnston, Alan Margolies, Gwen Nagel, and Alan Seaburg. Matthew J. Bruccoli has graciously allowed me to adapt the format used in the Pittsburgh Series of Bibliography, of which he is general editor.

I am fortunate to work at an institution that encourages and supports scholarship. I am grateful to the Department of English, George L. Geckle, chairman, for help. I also wish to thank the following research assistants: Caroline Bokinsky, Robert E. Burkholder, Robert Morace, and especially Stephen Garrison.

Greta has patiently endured the encroachment of Unitarian sermons on our shelves and time. I am grateful for her love and support.

Joel Myerson
Columbia, South Carolina
1 July 1981

NOTES

1. An argument could be made for extending the definition of *issue* in nineteenth-century books to include bindings as well. For example, sheets of the first printings of Parker's books (with the original title page) were often bound by Horace B. Fuller, in casings with his logo on the spine, for sale as part of his edition of [*Theodore Parker's Works*]. In such cases it is difficult to avoid regarding the new binding as an *issue* because it does represent a deliberate attempt to alter the conditions of publication.

2. G. Thomas Tanselle, "The Specifications of Binding Cloth," *The Library*, 21 (September 1966): 246–247. The reader should also consult Tanselle's excellent "The Bibliographical Description of Patterns," *Studies in Bibliography*, 23 (1970): 72–102, which reproduces all of the cloth grains illustrated in the *BAL* plus additional ones.

3. See G. Thomas Tanselle, "A System of Color Identification for Bibliographical Description," *Studies in Bibliography*, 20 (1967): 203–234, for a discussion of how this system can be fully employed. I feel, however, that the use of exact Centroid designations creates a false sense of precision, especially for nineteenth-century books. Oxidation, fading, wear, and nonuniform dyeing practices make precise color identification difficult, if not impossible. In any case, color identification by the Centroid system is inexact.

4. Parker's contributions to the *Dial* are listed in my "An Annotated List of Contributions to the Boston *Dial*," *Studies in Bibliography*, 26 (1973): 133–166. There is an incomplete handwritten list of Parker's contributions to the *Liberator* at the Library of Congress. Parker's contributions to the *Massachusetts Quarterly Review*, listed from his marked set of the journal, are described in Clarence L.F. Gohdes, *The Periodicals of American Transcendentalism* (Durham: Duke University Press, 1931). The bibliography by Charles W. Wendte in the *Centenary Edition* of Parker's works (see B 3) is still of use.

SECTION A:

SEPARATE PUBLICATIONS

A 1   THE PREVIOUS QUESTION BETWEEN MR. ANDREWS NORTON AND HIS
        ALUMNI
        1841

A 1

First edition, only printing (1840)

THE / PREVIOUS QUESTION / BETWEEN / MR. ANDREWS NORTON AND HIS
ALUMNI / MOVED AND HANDLED, / IN A / LETTER TO ALL THOSE
GENTLEMEN. / BY LEVI BLODGETT. / [rule] / BOSTON: / WEEKS, JORDAN,
AND COMPANY. / [rule] / 1840.

Pagination: [1-3] 4-24.

Collation: [1]^4 2-3^4.

Contents: p. 1: title page; p. 2: printer's imprint; pp. 3-24: text.

Typography and paper: page size: 9 7/16" X 5 11/16"; text size:
6 9/16" X 3 5/8"; wove paper; 40 lines per page. No running heads.

Binding: light gray wrappers: front recto: all within a double-rule
frame with an octagonal design in each corner: '[rule] / LEVI
BLODGETT / ON / THE PREVIOUS QUESTION / BETWEEN / MR. ANDREWS
NORTON AND HIS ALUMNI. / [rule]'; front verso and back recto and
verso: blank. All edges trimmed.

Printing: Freeman and Bolles, Washington Street, Boston.

Publication: MH copy (bound) received 1 May 1840.

Location: MHi.

4

A 2　　A DISCOURSE ON THE TRANSIENT AND PERMANENT IN CHRISTIANITY
1841

A 2.1

First edition, only printing (1841)

A / DISCOURSE / ON THE / TRANSIENT AND PERMANENT / [gothic] In
Christianity; / PREACHED AT THE ORDINATION OF / MR. CHARLES C.
SHACKFORD, / IN THE HAWES PLACE CHURCH IN BOSTON, / MAY 19, 1841. /
[rule] / BY THEODORE PARKER, / MINISTER OF THE SECOND CHURCH IN
ROXBURY. / [rule] / BOSTON: / PRINTED FOR THE AUTHOR. / [rule] /
MDCCCXLI.

Pagination: [1-5] 6-48.

Collation: $[1]^2$ 2-6^4 7^2.

Contents: p. 1: title page; p. 2: printer's imprint; p. 3:
'PREFACE.' dated 'WEST ROXBURY, June 17, 1841.'; p. 4: blank; pp.
5-48: text.

Typography and paper: page size: 9 1/8" X 5 7/8"; text size: 5 7/8"
X 3 7/16"; wove paper; 30 lines per page. No running heads.

Binding: light gray wrappers: front recto: all within a double-rule
frame with an octagonal ornament in each corner: '[rule] /
DISCOURSE / ON THE / TRANSIENT AND PERMANENT / IN / CHRISTIANITY. /
[rule]'; front verso and back recto and verso: blank. Untrimmed;
all edges trimmed.

Printing: Freeman and Bolles, Washington Street, Boston.

Publication: Unknown.

Locations: CtY, MH-AH.

Note: A copy has been located with a 12-line errata slip pasted in after p. 48: CtY.

A 2.2.a

Second edition, first printing (1841)

Title page: The same as in the first edition, except: 'A . . . 1841. / SECOND EDITION. / [rule] . . . MDCCCXLI.'.

39pp. (30pp. of text and a nine-page 'APPENDIX TO THE SECOND EDITION.'). Wrappers. *Locations:* BL, MH, MH-AH.

A 2.2.b

Second edition, second printing (1841)

Title page: The same as in the first edition, except: 'A . . . PERMANENT / IN CHRISTIANITY; / PREACHED . . . 1841. / THIRD EDITION. / [rule] / BY . . . BOSTON: / B. H. GREENE AND E. P. PEABODY. / [rule] / M DCCC XLI.'.

30pp. *Location:* MH.

A 2.3.a-b

Third edition, first and second printings [1885?]

Title page: [printed in a curved line] FREEDOM, FELLOWSHIP AND CHARACTER IN RELIGION. / Unity Mission / No. 36. / Single copies, 5 cts.; 10 copies, 25 cts. / UNITY OFFICE, 175 DEARBORN STREET, CHICAGO. / THE TRANSIENT AND PERMANENT IN / CHRISTIANITY. / [rule] / BY THEODORE PARKER. / [rule] / A SERMON PREACHED AT THE ORDINATION OF CHARLES C. SHACKFORD, IN SOUTH BOSTON, MAY 19, 1841. / [20 lines, double columns, introduction] / *Heaven and earth shall pass away; but my word shall not pass away.*—LUKE XXI.33. / [10 lines of text in double columns]

17pp. Head title. *Unity Mission*, no. 36. Price, 5¢. *Locations:* MH-AH (2d thousand), RPB (2d thousand).

Note: No copies of the first printing have been located.

A 2.4.a–p

Fourth edition, first through sixteenth printings [1907–1928]

Title page: [MEMORABLE SERMONS, NO. 10] / THE TRANSIENT AND
PERMANENT / IN CHRISTIANITY / THEODORE PARKER / PUBLISHED FOR FREE
DISTRIBUTION / AMERICAN UNITARIAN ASSOCIATION / 25 BEACON STREET,
BOSTON

34pp. Cover title. First printing, May 1907. *Memorable Sermons*,
no. 10. *Locations:* JM (1907), MH–AH (14th printing, September
1926), MH–AH (16th printing, December 1928).

A 2.5.a–b

Fifth edition, first and second printings [1941–1942]

Title page: THE TRANSIENT AND / PERMANENT IN CHRISTIANITY / [rule] /
· *by* THEODORE PARKER · / [rule] / 1810–1860 / CENTENARY EDITION /
No. "D" / AMERICAN UNITARIAN ASSOCIATION / [rule] / 25 BEACON
STREET · BOSTON, MASSACHUSETTS

39pp. Wrappers. Introduction by John Hayne Holmes. *Great
Unitarian Churchmen*, no. D. Printed from the *Centenary Edition*
plates (see B 3). First printing, May 1941. *Locations:* MH–AH
(1941), ViU (2d printing, January 1942).

A 2.5.c

Fifth edition, third printing (1948)

Title page: The Transient / *and Permanent* / *in Christianity* / By /
THEODORE PARKER / [publisher's logo] / Boston · THE BEACON PRESS ·
1948

39pp. Wrappers. *Beacon Reference Series.* Price, 25¢. *Location:*
CtY.

A 3   LECTURE ON THE EDUCATION OF THE LABORING CLASS
1842?

A 3

First edition, only printing [1842?]

LECTURE / ON THE / EDUCATION OF THE LABORING CLASS. / [rule] / BY
THEODORE PARKER. / [rule] / [18 lines of text]

Pagination: [1] 2–26.

Collation: 1–2^6 [3]^1.

Contents: pp. 1–26: text.

Typography and paper: page size: 7 5/16" X 4 5/8"; text size:
5 3/4" (5 1/2") X 3 1/4"; wove paper; 39 lines per page. Running
heads: rectos: pp. 3–25: 'EDUCATION OF THE LABORING CLASS.';
versos: pp. 2–24: 'MR. PARKER'S LECTURE ON THE'; p. 26: 'MR.
PARKER'S LECTURE.'.

Binding: Head title. All edges trimmed.

Printing: Unknown.

Publication: MH copy (bound) received from Convers Francis 24 March
1843.

Location: MH.

Note one: The only located copy has been bound into a volume with
other pamphlets; therefore, pagination, collation, contents, page
size, and binding information are conjectural.

Note two: Reprinted from the plates of *The Lectures Delivered Before
the American Institute of Instruction, at Boston, August 1841 . . .*
(Boston: William D. Ticknor, 1842), pp. 65–90.

8

A 4   A DISCOURSE OF MATTERS PERTAINING TO RELIGION
         1842

A 4.1.a

First edition, first printing (1842)

A / DISCOURSE / OF / MATTERS PERTAINING TO RELIGION. / BY / THEODORE
PARKER, / MINISTER OF THE SECOND CHURCH IN ROXBURY, MASS. / [two
lines from Jerome] / BOSTON: / CHARLES C. LITTLE AND JAMES BROWN. /
MDCCCXLII.

Pagination: [i-iii] iv [v] vi-vii [viii] [1-3] 4-7 [8-11] 12-19 [20]
21-28 [29] 30-43 [44] 45-50 [51] 52-111 [112] 113-131 [132] 133-155
[156-159] 160-169 [170] 171-180 [181] 182 [183] 184-189 [190]
191-196 [197] 198-206 [207] 208-214 [215] 216-234 [235-237] 238-245
[246] 247-252 [253] 254-261 [262] 263-280 [281] 282-288 [289]
290-298 [299] 300-314 [315-317] 318-326 [327] 328-350 [351] 352-363
[364] 365-368 [369] 370-377 [378-381] 382-387 [388] 389-404 [405]
406-407 [408] 409-435 [436] 437-476 [477] 478-481 [482] 483-485
[486-489] 490-504.

Collation: [a]^4 1-63^4.

Contents: p. i: title page; p. ii: copyright information and
printer's imprint; pp. iii-iv: 'THE PREFACE.' dated 'WEST ROXBURY,
MASS. / 7th MAY, 1842.'; pp. v-vii: contents; p. viii: blank; p. 1:
'THE INTRODUCTION.'; p. 2: 20 lines from Andrews Norton; pp. 3-7:
introduction; p. 8: blank; p. 9: 'BOOK I.'; p. 10: 16 lines from
John Locke; pp. 11-155: "Book I. Of Religion in General; or A
Discourse of the Religious Sentiment and Its Manifestations"; p.
156: blank; p. 157: 'BOOK II.'; p. 158: 10 lines from John Locke;
pp. 159-234: "Book II. The Relation of the Religious Sentiment to
God, or A Discourse of Inspiration"; p. 235: 'BOOK III.'; p. 236:
nine lines from Samuel Taylor Coleridge and eight lines from Seneca;
pp. 237-314: "Book III. The Relation of the Religious Sentiment to
Jesus of Nazareth, or A Discourse of Christianity"; p. 315: 'BOOK
IV.'; p. 316: 20 lines from "G. B."; pp. 317-377: "Book IV. The

Relation of the Religious Sentiment to the Greatest of Books, or A Discourse of the Bible"; p. 378: blank; p. 379: 'BOOK V.'; p. 380: 20 lines from John Milton; pp. 381–485: "Book V. The Relation of the Religious Sentiment to the Greatest of Human Institutions, or A Discourse of the Church"; p. 486: blank; p. 487: 'THE CONCLUSION.'; p. 488: 14 lines from Andrews Norton and 14 lines from Ralph Waldo Emerson; pp. 489–504: "The Conclusion."

Typography and paper: page size: 9 1/16" X 5 5/8"; text size: 6 3/8" (6 1/8") X 3 7/16"; wove paper; 31 lines per page. Running heads: rectos and versos: topical headings.

Binding: black T cloth (rib); front and back covers: blindstamped triple-rule frame with 7" X 4" double bands and leaf-and-vine ornament in center; spine: blindstamped ornate bands with goldstamped 'PARKER'S / DISCOURSE / OF / RELIGION.'. Flyleaves. White endpapers. All edges trimmed.

Printing: Freeman and Bolles, Washington Street, Boston.

Publication: Parker wrote in his journal on 6 May 1842: "To-day I received the last proof-sheet" (Weiss, *Life and Correspondence* [C 5], 1:183). Deposited for copyright: title, 10 May 1842; book, 21 May 1842. Inscribed copy: MH-AH (July 1842).

Locations: JM, MB, MH-AH.

Note: A copy has been noted with a 30-line errata slip pasted to the front flyleaf verso: MB. Parker wrote a friend on 10 October 1842 that a list of six or eight errata was printed "in about a fortnight" of publication, and that "some *weeks* later" he had printed "a more complete list of them" (Weiss, *Life and Correspondence* [C 5], 1:188).

A 4.1.b

First edition, second printing (1843)

Title page: The same as in the first printing, except: 'A . . .
BROWN. / MDCCCXLIII.'.

504pp. *Location:* BL (rebound).

Note: The only located copy has a 30-line errata slip inserted after
p. 504.

A 4.1.c

First edition, third (English) printing (1844)

Title page: The same as in the first printing, except: 'A . . .
[two lines from Jerome] / LONDON: / JOHN CHAPMAN, 121, NEWGATE
STREET. / [rule] / M.DCCC.XLIV.'.

504pp. Price, 14s. *Location:* InU (rebound).

Note: Possibly an English issue of the American sheets with a cancel
title leaf, but, because the only located copy has been rebound,
this cannot be determined.

A 4.1.d

First edition, fourth printing (1972)

Title page: A / DISCOURSE / OF / MATTERS PERTAINING TO RELIGION /
BY / THEODORE PARKER / ['NYT' logo] / ARNO PRESS / A NEW YORK TIMES
COMPANY / New York · 1972

504pp. Facsimile reprinting. Price, $24.00. *Locations:* NjP, ScU.

A 4.2

First English edition, only printing (1846)

A / DISCOURSE OF MATTERS / PERTAINING TO / RELIGION. / BY / THEODORE
PARKER, / MINISTER OF THE SECOND CHURCH IN ROXBURY, MASS. / [two
lines from Jerome] / LONDON: / CHAPMAN, BROTHERS, 121, NEWGATE
STREET. / [rule] / M.DCCC.XLVI.

Pagination: [i-v] vi [vii] viii [1-3] 4-6 [7-9] 10-116 [117-119]
120-174 [175-177] 178-234 [235-237] 238-282 [283-285] 286-365
[366-369] 370-380.

Collation: [a]^2 b^2 A-I^6 K-U^6 X-Z^6 Aa-Hh^6 Ii^4.

Contents: p. i: 'A / DISCOURSE OF MATTERS / PERTAINING TO /
RELIGION.'; p. ii: blank; p. iii: title page; p. iv: blank; pp.
v-vi: 'THE PREFACE.'; pp. vii-viii: contents; pp. 1-380: text.

Typography and paper: page size: 7 11/16" X 4 5/8"; text size:
5 3/4" (5 1/2") X 3 3/16"; wove paper; 36 lines per page. Running
heads: rectos: pp. 5-379: topical headings; versos: p. vi:
'PREFACE.'; p. viii: 'CONTENTS.'; pp. 4-380: topical headings.

Binding: black T cloth (rib); front and back covers: blindstamped
single-rule frame with 2 1/4" leaf-and-vine design in each corner
and 3 5/8" leaf-and-vine design in center; spine: blindstamped rules
with goldstamped 'PARKER'S / DISCOURSE / OF / RELIGION / LONDON. /
JOHN CHAPMAN.'. Light brown; pale yellow; pale yellow coated
endpapers. All edges trimmed.

Printing: Robert Hardie and Company, Edinburgh.

Publication: Probably published in the fall of 1846; see the Note to
A 4.3. Price, 7s.

Location: KyLxCB.

Note one: A copy has been noted with a 32-page catalogue of John Chapman's publications, dated 12 January 1848, inserted at the back: KyLxCB.

Note two: A copy has been noted with a 24-page catalogue of John Chapman's publications, dated May 1849, inserted at the back: BE (spine defective).

Note three: A copy has been noted with a 24-page catalogue of John Chapman's publications, dated September 1850, inserted at the back: MB (spine defective).

A 4.3
Third edition, only printing (1847)

Title page: A / DISCOURSE / OF / MATTERS PERTAINING TO RELIGION, / BY / THEODORE PARKER. / [two lines from Jerome] / [rule] / THIRD EDITION. / [rule] / BOSTON: / CHARLES C. LITTLE AND JAMES BROWN. / [rule] / M.DCCC.XLVII.

472pp. *Locations:* JM, MH, MH-AH.

Note: The "Preface," dated 25 December 1846, states "The second edition of this Discourse was published at London a few months ago . . ." (p. [vii]).

A 4.4.a
Fourth (English) edition, first printing (1849)

Title page: A / DISCOURSE OF MATTERS / PERTAINING TO / RELIGION. / BY / THEODORE PARKER, / MINISTER OF THE SECOND CHURCH IN ROXBURY, MASS. / [two lines from Jerome] / LONDON: / J. WATSON, QUEEN'S HEAD PASSAGE, PATERNOSTER ROW. / WORTLEY: / PRINTED BY JOSEPH BARKER. / [rule] / MDCCCXLIX.

320pp. *Location:* BO.

A 4.4.b

Fourth (English) edition, second printing (1850)

Title page: The same as in the fourth edition, first printing, except: 'A . . . MDCCCL.'.

320pp. *Location:* MB.

A 4.5

Fifth (English) edition, only printing (1852)

Title page: A / DISCOURSE OF MATTERS / PERTAINING TO / RELIGION. / BY / THEODORE PARKER, / MINISTER OF THE SECOND CHURCH IN ROXBURY, MASS. / [two lines from Jerome] / LONDON: / JOHN CHAPMAN, 142. STRAND. / [rule] / M.DCCC.LII.

309pp. *The Catholic Series.* Deposit copy: BL (16 September 1852). Price, 4s. *Location:* BL.

A 4.6.a

Sixth edition, first printing (1856)

Title page: A / DISCOURSE / OF / MATTERS PERTAINING TO RELIGION. / BY / THEODORE PARKER. / [rule] / [two lines from Jerome] / [rule] / FOURTH EDITION. / BOSTON: / LITTLE, BROWN AND COMPANY. / 1856.

466pp. Inscribed copy: MH (from Parker, 22 February 1856). *Locations:* CtY, MH, MH-AH.

Note: The "Preface" is dated 25 December 1855 (p. vii). Parker wrote S. J. May on 11 February 1856 that the "new edition" was out, in which "I have made some alterations of considerable importance" (Weiss, *Life and Correspondence* [C 5], 1:323).

A 4.6.b

Sixth edition, second printing (1864)

Title page: The same as in the sixth edition, first printing, except: 'A . . . EDITION. / NEW YORK: / PUBLISHED BY D. APPLETON & CO. / BOSTON: / T. O. H. P. BURNHAM. / 1864.'.

466pp. Noted in *[Theodore Parker's Works]* binding (see B 2), but without any publisher's stamping at the bottom of the spine. *Locations:* MH, MWA.

A 4.6.c

Sixth edition, third printing (1870)

Title page: The same as in the sixth edition, first printing, except: 'A . . . [two lines from Jerome] / [rule] / FIFTH EDITION. / BOSTON: / HORACE B. FULLER, / 14, BROMFIELD STREET. / 1870.'.

466pp. Noted in *[Theodore Parker's Works]* binding (see B 2). Price, $1.50. *Locations:* JM, ViU.

A 4.6.d

Sixth edition, fourth printing (1876)

Title page: A DISCOURSE / OF / MATTERS PERTAINING TO RELIGION / BY / THEODORE PARKER / [two lines from Jerome] / *FOURTH EDITION* / WITH AN INTRODUCTION BY / OCTAVIUS BROOKS FROTHINGHAM / AND A BIOGRAPHICAL SKETCH BY / HANNAH E. STEVENSON / NEW YORK / G. P. PUTNAM'S SONS / 182 FIFTH AVENUE / 1876

466pp. Price, $1.50. *Location:* JM.

A 4.7.a

Seventh (English) edition, first printing (1863)

Title page: A / DISCOURSE / OF / MATTERS PERTAINING TO RELIGION. / BY / THEODORE PARKER. / [two lines from Jerome] / LONDON: / TRÜBNER & CO., 60, PATERNOSTER ROW. / 1863.

335pp. Preface by Frances Power Cobbe. *Collected Works*, vol. 1 (see B 1). Deposit copy: BL (9 February 1863). Price, 6s. *Locations:* BE, BL, BO, NcU.

A 4.7.b

Seventh (English) edition, second printing (1872)

Title page: The same as in the seventh edition, first printing, except: 'A . . . LONDON: / N. TRÜBNER & CO., 60, PATERNOSTER ROW. / 1872.'.

335pp. Wrappers. *People's Edition.* Deposit copy: BL (21 July 1874). Price, 1s6d. *Location:* BL.

A 4.7.c

Seventh (English) edition, third printing (1876)

Title page: The same as in the seventh edition, first printing, except: 'A . . . LONDON: / TRÜBNER & CO., LUDGATE HILL. / 1876.'.

335pp. *Collected Works*, vol. 1 (see B 1). *Location:* JM.

A 4.7.d

Seventh (English) edition, fourth printing (1881)

Title page: The same as in the seventh edition, third printing, except: 'A . . . HILL. / 1881.'.

335pp. *Location:* MH-AH.

A 4.8.a

Eighth (English) edition, first printing (1873)

Title page: A DISCOURSE / OF MATTERS / PERTAINING TO RELIGION. /
BY / THEODORE PARKER. / [gothic] With a Preface / BY THE REV.
CHARLES VOYSEY, B.A., / *Late Vicar of Healaugh.* / [rule] / [two
lines from Jerome] / [rule] / *LONDON:* / LONGMANS, GREEN, READER,
AND DYER. / 1873.

295pp. Deposit copy: BL (20 June 1873). Price, 3s. *Locations:*
BE, BL.

A 4.8.b

Eighth (English) edition, second printing (1875)

Title page: The same as in the eighth edition, first printing,
except: 'A . . . DYER. / 1875.'.

295pp. *Location:* ICN.

A 4.9

Ninth edition, only printing [1907]

Title page: A DISCOURSE / OF / MATTERS PERTAINING TO / RELIGION /
BY / THEODORE PARKER / EDITED WITH A PREFACE / BY / THOMAS
WENTWORTH HIGGINSON / [two lines from Jerome] / [publisher's logo] /
BOSTON / AMERICAN UNITARIAN ASSOCIATION / 25 BEACON STREET

451pp. *Centenary Edition*, vol. [1] (see B 3). Deposited for
copyright, 25 November 1907. MH-AH copy received 14 January 1908.
Price, $1.00. *Locations:* InU, JM, MBAt, MH, MH-AH, NcU.

A 5   AN HUMBLE TRIBUTE TO THE MEMORY OF WILLIAM ELLERY CHANNING
1842

A 5.1

First edition, only printing (1842)

AN / HUMBLE TRIBUTE / TO THE MEMORY OF / WILLIAM ELLERY CHANNING,
D. D. / [rule] / A / SERMON / PREACHED AT WEST ROXBURY, OCTOBER
9th, 1842, / BY THEODORE PARKER, / MINISTER OF THE SECOND CHURCH IN
ROXBURY. / PRINTED BY REQUEST. / [rule] / BOSTON: / CHARLES C.
LITTLE AND JAMES BROWN. / 1842.

Pagination: [1-5] 6-38 [39-40].

Collation: [1]^4 2-5^4.

Contents: p. 1: title page; p. 2: printer's imprint; p. 3:
'PREFACE.' dated 'WEST ROXBURY, OCT. 12, 1842.'; p. 4: blank; pp.
5-38: text; pp. 39-40: blank.

Typography and paper: page size: 8 11/16" X 5 5/8"; text size:
6 1/8" X 3 3/8"; wove paper; 31 lines per page. No running heads.

Binding: light brown wrappers: front recto: all within a double-rule
frame: '[rule] / AN / HUMBLE TRIBUTE / TO THE MEMORY OF / WILLIAM
E. CHANNING, D. D. / [rule]'; front verso and back recto and verso:
blank. All edges trimmed.

Printing: Freeman and Bolles, Washington Street, Boston.

Publication: MH copy received 20 March 1843.

Locations: MH, MH-AH.

18

A 5.2

First English edition, only printing (1842)

AN / HUMBLE TRIBUTE / TO THE MEMORY OF / WILLIAM ELLERY CHANNING, D. D. / [rule] / A SERMON / PREACHED AT WEST ROXBURY, OCTOBER 9TH, 1842. / BY / THEODORE PARKER, / MINISTER OF THE SECOND CHURCH IN ROXBURY. / LONDON: / JOHN GREEN, 121, NEWGATE STREET. / [rule] / MDCCCXLII.

Pagination: [1-3] 4-24.

Collation: [A]^8 B^4.

Contents: p. 1: title page; p. 2: printer's imprint; pp. 3-24: text.

Typography and paper: page size: 8 1/2" X 5 1/2"; text size: 6 1/2" X 3 5/8"; wove paper; 40 lines per page. No running heads.

Binding: light gray wrappers: front recto: the same as the title page within a single-rule frame, with '[PRICE ONE SHILLING.]' below the frame; front verso and back recto and verso: blank. All edges trimmed.

Printing: Richard Kinder, Green Arbour Court, Old Bailey, London.

Publication: Price, 1s.

Location: NN.

A 6   CRITICAL AND MISCELLANEOUS WRITINGS
        1843

A 6.1.

First edition, only printing (1843)

THE / CRITICAL AND MISCELLANEOUS / WRITINGS / OF / THEODORE
PARKER, / MINISTER OF THE SECOND CHURCH IN ROXBURY. / [rule] /
BOSTON: / JAMES MUNROE AND COMPANY. / LONDON: / JOHN GREEN, 121
NEWGATE STREET. / 1843.

Pagination: [i–viii] [1] 2–360.

Collation: [a]^4 1–30^6.

Contents: p. i: 'PARKER'S / CRITICAL AND MISCELLANEOUS / WRITINGS.';
p. ii: blank; p. iii: title page; p. iv: copyright information and
printer's imprint; p. v: 'PREFACE.' dated 'WEST ROXBURY, Dec. 28th,
1842.'; p. vi: blank; p. vii: contents; p. viii: blank; pp. 1–24:
"A Lesson for the Day"; pp. 25–54: "German Literature"; pp. 55–106:
"The Life of St. Bernard of Clairvaux"; pp. 107–108: "Truth Against
the World"; pp. 109–135: "Thoughts on Labor"; pp. 136–169: "A
Discourse of the Transient and Permanent in Christianity"; pp.
170–191: "The Pharisees"; pp. 192–219: "On the Education of the
Laboring Classes"; pp. 220–221: "How to Move the World"; pp.
222–247: "Primitive Christianity"; pp. 248–308: "Strauss's Life of
Jesus"; pp. 309–360: "Thoughts on Theology."

Typography and paper: page size: 7 9/16" X 4 5/8"; text size: 5 7/8"
(5 5/8") X 3 1/4"; wove paper; 35 lines per page. Running heads:
rectos and versos: chapter titles.

Binding: Four styles have been noted, priority undetermined:

> *Binding A:* black T cloth (rib); front and back covers:
> blindstamped triple-rule frame with lines connecting the
> corners of the second and third frames, outside of a

single-rule frame with intersecting lines in each corner, with a 4 1/2" leaf-and-vine ornament in the center; spine: blindstamped rules with goldstamped 'PARKER'S / MISCELLANEOUS / WRITINGS'. Flyleaves. Cream coated endpapers. All edges trimmed.

Binding B: dark brown L cloth (morocco); gray green T cloth (rib); front and back covers: blindstamped triple-rule frame with a 7 3/8" leaf-and-vine design in the center; spine: blindstamped ornamental bands with goldstamped 'PARKER'S / MISCELLANEOUS / WRITINGS'. Flyleaves. White endpapers. All edges trimmed.

Binding C: black T cloth (rib); front and back covers: blindstamped quintuple-rule frame with leafy ornaments inside the corners and sides; spine: blindstamped bands with goldstamped 'CRITICAL / AND / MISCELLANEOUS / WRITINGS / [rule] / PARKER.'. Flyleaves. Yellow endpapers. All edges trimmed.

Binding D: dark brown L cloth (morocco); front and back covers: blindstamped triple-rule frame with lines connecting the corners of the second and third frames, outside of a single-rule frame with intersecting lines in each corner, with a 3 1/2" floral ornament in the center; spine: blindstamped bands with goldstamped 'PARKER'S / MISCELLANEOUS / WRITINGS'. Flyleaves. Pale pink endpapers. All edges trimmed.

Printing: Thurston and Torrey, Boston.

Publication: Inscribed copy: MB (rebound; from Parker, 31 December 1842).

Locations: Binding A: JM; Binding B: CSt, JM, MH; Binding C: BL; Binding D: MBAt.

Printing histories: "A Lesson for the Day," *Dial*, 1 (October 1840): 196–216; "German Literature," *Dial*, 1 (January 1841): 315–339; "The Life of St. Bernard of Clairvaux," *Christian Examiner*, 30 (March 1841): 1–41; "Truth Against the World," *Dial*, 1 (October 1840): 218–219; "Thoughts on Labor," *Dial*, 1 (April 1841): 497–519; "A Discourse of the Transient and Permanent in Christianity," see A 2; "The Pharisees," *Dial*, 2 (July 1841): 59–76; "On the Education of the Laboring Classes," see A 3; "How to Move the World," unlocated; "Primitive Christianity," *Dial*, 2 (January 1842): 292–313; "Strauss's Life of Jesus," *Christian Examiner*, 28 (June 1840): 273–317; "Thoughts on Theology," *Dial*, 2 (April 1842): 485–528.

A 6.2

First English edition, only printing (1848)

THE / CRITICAL / AND / MISCELLANEOUS WRITINGS / OF / THEODORE
PARKER, / MINISTER OF THE SECOND CHURCH IN ROXBURY, MASS. /
LONDON: / JOHN CHAPMAN, 142, STRAND. / [rule] / MDCCCXLVIII.

Pagination: [i–iv] [1] 2–177 [178] 179–334.

Collation: [A]^2 B–I^{12} K–P^{12} $_{(-P_{12})}$.

Contents: p. i: '[gothic] The Catholic Series. / [three–line blurb
for the series]'; p. ii: blank; p. iii: title page; p. iv: printer's
imprint; pp. 1–334: text.

Typography and paper: page size: 7 13/16" X 4 3/4"; text size:
5 13/16" (5 9/16") X 3 3/16"; wove paper; 37 lines per page.
Running heads: rectos and versos: topical headings.

Binding: dark brown T cloth (rib); front and back covers:
blindstamped ornate frame with a 2 1/2" circular "The Catholic
Series" ornament in the center; spine: blindstamped rules with
goldstamped 'PARKER'S / MISCELLANEOUS / WRITINGS / LONDON. / JOHN
CHAPMAN.'. Yellow; pale yellow endpapers. All edges trimmed.

Printing: Richard Kinder, Green Arbour Court, Old Bailey, London.

Publication: The Catholic Series. Price, 7s.

Locations: BE, BO.

Note one: A copy has been noted with a 24–page catalogue of John
Chapman's publications, dated January 1849, inserted at the back:
BE.

Note two: A copy has been noted with a 24–page catalogue of John
Chapman's publications, dated January 1849, followed by a 24–page

catalogue of Chapman's American books, dated March 1849, inserted
at the back: BO.

A 6.3.a

Third edition, first printing (1856)

Title page: THE / CRITICAL AND MISCELLANEOUS / WRITINGS / OF /
THEODORE PARKER, / MINISTER OF THE TWENTY-EIGHTH CONGREGATIONAL
SOCIETY IN BOSTON. / SECOND EDITION. / BOSTON: / LITTLE, BROWN AND
COMPANY. / 1856.

400pp. Price, $1.25. *Locations:* CSt, CtY, TxU.

A 6.3.b

Third edition, second printing (1859)

Title page: The same as in the third edition, first printing,
except: 'THE . . . BOSTON: / RUFUS LEIGHTON, JR. / 1859.'.

400pp. *Location:* RPB.

A 6.3.c

Third edition, third printing (1864)

Title page: The same as in the third edition, first printing,
except: 'THE . . . EDITION. / NEW YORK: / D. APPLETON AND COMPANY. /
BOSTON: T. O. H. P. BURNHAM. / 1864.'.

400pp. *Location:* NIC (rebound).

A 6.3.d

Third edition, fourth printing (1867)

Title page: The same as in the third edition, first printing,
except: 'THE . . . BOSTON: / HORACE B. FULLER / (SUCCESSOR TO
WALKER, FULLER, AND COMPANY,) / 245, WASHINGTON STREET. / 1867.'.

400pp. Noted in *[Theodore Parker's Works]* binding (see B 2).
Price, $1.50. *Locations:* NjP, ViU.

A 6.3.e
Third edition, fifth printing [1870]

Title page: The same as in the third edition, first printing,
except: 'THE / CRITICAL AND MISCELLANEOUS / WRITINGS . . .
BOSTON. / BOSTON. / HORACE B. FULLER. / 14 BROMFIELD STREET.

400pp. Noted in *[Theodore Parker's Works]* binding (see B 2).
Price, $1.50. *Location:* JM.

A 7   A SERMON OF SLAVERY
1843

A 7

First edition, only printing (1843)

A / SERMON OF SLAVERY, / DELIVERED JAN. 31, 1841, REPEATED JUNE 4, 1843, / AND NOW / PUBLISHED BY REQUEST; / BY / THEODORE PARKER, / MINISTER OF THE SECOND CHURCH IN ROXBURY. / [rule] / BOSTON: / PRINTED BY THURSTON AND TORREY. / M DCCC XLIII.

Pagination: [1-3] 4-24.

Collation: [1]^6 2^6.

Contents: p. 1: title page; p. 2: copyright information; pp. 3-24: text.

Typography and paper: page size: 7 11/16" X 4 3/4"; text size: 5 9/16" (5 5/16") X 3"; wove paper; 32 lines per page. Running heads: rectos and versos: 'SERMON OF SLAVERY.'.

Binding: medium brown wrappers: front recto: the same as the title page within a single-rule frame with floral designs in each corner; front verso and back recto and verso: blank. All edges trimmed.

Printing: Thurston and Torrey, Boston.

Publication: Deposited for copyright: title, 19 June 1843; book, 14 August 1843. MH copy received 21 June 1843. Deposit copy: DLC (14 August 1843).

Locations: DLC, MH, MH-AH.

A 8   THE RELATION OF JESUS TO HIS AGE AND THE AGES
1845

A 8

First edition, only printing (1845)

THE RELATION OF JESUS TO HIS AGE AND THE AGES. / [rule] / A / SERMON / PREACHED AT / THE THURSDAY LECTURE, / IN BOSTON. / DECEMBER 26, 1844. / [rule] / BY THEODORE PARKER, / MINISTER OF THE SECOND CHURCH IN ROXBURY. / [rule] / BOSTON: / CHARLES C. LITTLE AND JAMES BROWN. / MDCCCXLV.

Pagination: [1–3] 4–18 [19–20].

Collation: [1–2^4] 3^2.

Contents: p. 1: title page; p. 2: copyright information and printer's imprint; pp. 3–18: text; pp. 19–20: blank.

Typography and paper: page size: 8 5/8" X 5 3/8"; text size: 6 5/16" X 3 5/8"; wove paper; 34 lines per page. No running heads.

Binding: light brown wrappers: front recto: all within a double-rule frame: '[wavy rule] / MR. PARKER'S SERMON / ON / THE RELATION OF JESUS TO HIS AGE / AND / THE AGES. / [wavy rule]'; front verso and back recto and verso: blank. All edges trimmed.

Printing: Freeman and Bolles, Washington Street, Boston.

Publication: Unknown.

Locations: JM, MH–AH, TxU.

A 9   THE EXCELLENCE OF GOODNESS
        1845

A 9

First edition, only printing (1845)

THE EXCELLENCE OF GOODNESS. / [rule] / A / SERMON / PREACHED IN /
THE CHURCH OF THE DISCIPLES, / IN BOSTON, / ON SUNDAY, JANUARY 26,
1845. / [rule] / BY THEODORE PARKER, / MINISTER OF THE SECOND CHURCH
IN ROXBURY. / [rule] / PUBLISHED BY REQUEST. / BOSTON / BENJAMIN H.
GREENE. / [rule] / MDCCCXLV.

Pagination: [1–3] 4–16.

Collation: $[1]^4 2^4$.

Contents: p. 1: title page; p. 2: copyright information and
printer's imprint; pp. 3–16: text.

Typography and paper: page size: 8 13/16" X 5 9/16"; text size:
6 5/16" X 3 11/16"; wove paper; 35 lines per page. No running
heads.

Binding: light orange–brown wrappers; front recto: all within a
double–rule frame: '[wavy rule] / MR. PARKER'S SERMON / ON THE /
EXCELLENCE OF GOODNESS. / [wavy rule]'; front verso and back recto
and verso: blank. All edges trimmed.

Printing: Freeman and Bolles, Washington Street, Boston.

Publication: Deposited for copyright: title, 12 February 1845.

Locations: JM, MH, MH–AH.

A 10   A LETTER TO THE BOSTON ASSOCIATION OF CONGREGATIONAL
        MINISTERS
        1845

A 10.1
First edition, only printing (1845)

A / LETTER / TO THE / BOSTON ASSOCIATION / OF / CONGREGATIONAL
MINISTERS, / TOUCHING CERTAIN MATTERS OF THEIR THEOLOGY. / [rule] /
BY THEODORE PARKER, / MINISTER OF THE SECOND CHURCH IN ROXBURY. /
[rule] / BOSTON: / CHARLES C. LITTLE AND JAMES BROWN. / [rule] /
MDCCCXLV.

Pagination: [1–3] 4–20.

Collation: [1]^4 2^4 3^2.

Contents: p. 1: title page; p. 2: printer's imprint; pp. 3–20:
text, signed 'THEODORE PARKER. / WEST ROXBURY, March 20th, 1845.'.

Typography and paper: page size: 9 1/8'' X 5 9/16''; text size: 6 3/8''
X 3 1/2''; wove paper; 34 lines per page. No running heads.

Binding: light tan; pale yellow wrappers; front recto: all within a
double-rule frame: '[wavy rule] / MR. PARKER'S LETTER / TO / THE
BOSTON ASSOCIATION / OF / CONGREGATIONAL MINISTERS. / [wavy rule]';
front verso and back recto and verso: blank. All edges trimmed.

Printing: Freeman and Bolles, Washington Street, Boston.

Publication: Unknown.

Locations: BL, CtY, MH, MH-AH, MHi.

Note one: Copies have been noted with a slip reading 'POSTSCRIPT. /
Since printing the above Letter I have received a note from Mr. /
Pierpont, correcting the statement on p. 10. He informs me that /

Messrs. Gannett, Sargent and Waterston have exchanged with him, /
and that Messrs. Clarke and Bartol have offered an exchange, since /
the termination of the Hollis Street Council.' pasted to the front
wrapper verso (BL) or on p. 20 (MH).

Note two: The following reading is present at 10.1–6: ' . . .
fellowship to / me — Mr. Pierpont, Mr. Sargent and Mr. Clarke, — /
only three, — Mr. Gannett, Mr. Sargent and Mr. / Clarke, — if I am
rightly informed, have extended / that fellowship to him since the
time of the famed Hollis-Street Council! . . .'.

A 10.2
Second edition, only printing (1845)

Title page: The same as in the first edition, except: 'A . . .
ROXBURY. / [rule] / SECOND EDITION. / BOSTON: . . .'.

20pp. Wrappers. *Locations:* JM, MBAt, MH-AH, MHi.

Note: The following reading is present at 10.1–7: ' . . .
fellowship / to me — Mr. Pierpont, Mr. Sargent, and Mr. /
Clarke, — only three, — Mr. Gannett, Mr. Sargent / and Mr.
Waterston — if I am rightly informed, have / actually extended
that fellowship to him since the time / of the famed Hollis-Street
Council, though Messrs. / Clarke and Bartol have offered
exchanges! . . .'. For the background to this revision, see Note
One for A 10.1. Other revisions are also present in the second
edition.

A 11   THE IDEA OF A CHRISTIAN CHURCH
          1846

A 11

First edition, only printing (1846)

THE IDEA OF A CHRISTIAN CHURCH. / [rule] / A / DISCOURSE / AT THE /
INSTALLATION OF THEODORE PARKER / AS MINISTER / OF THE /
TWENTY-EIGHTH CONGREGATIONAL CHURCH / IN BOSTON, / JANUARY 4,
1846. / DELIVERED BY HIMSELF. / [rule] / Published by the Request
of the Society. / [rule] / BOSTON: / PUBLISHED BY BENJ. H. GREENE. /
[rule] / PRINTED BY I. R. BUTTS. / 1846.

Pagination: [1-3] 4-36 [37] 38-39 [40].

Collation: [1]^4 2-5^4.

Contents: p. 1: title page; p. 2: blank; pp. 3-36: text; pp. 37-39:
'APPENDIX.'; p. 40: blank.

Typography and paper: page size: 9 5/16" X 5 3/4"; text size:
6 7/16" X 3 5/8"; wove paper; text: 33 lines per page; appendix:
various lines per page. No running heads.

Binding: Two styles have been noted, priority undetermined:

> *Binding A:* light tan wrappers: front recto: all within a
> triple-rule frame with a design in each corner: the same as
> the title page, except: 'THE . . . BOSTON: / PUBLISHED BY
> B. H. GREENE. / [rule] . . .'; front verso and back recto
> and verso: blank. All edges trimmed.

> *Binding B:* the same as Binding A, except: light gray; light
> tan wrappers; front recto reads 'BOSTON'.

Printing: I. R. Butts, Boston.

Publication: For evidence that the discourse was published by 21 March 1846, see Weiss, *Life and Correspondence* (C 5), 1:317. Inscribed copy: JM (22 July 1846).

Locations: Binding A: JM; Binding B: MH–AH.

A 12   A SERMON OF WAR
           1846

A 12.1

First edition, only printing (1846)

A / SERMON OF WAR, / PREACHED AT THE / MELODEON, / ON SUNDAY, JUNE
7, 1846. / BY / THEODORE PARKER, / MINISTER OF THE TWENTY-EIGHTH
CONGREGATIONAL CHURCH IN BOSTON. / [rule] / PUBLISHED BY REQUEST. /
[rule] / BOSTON: / CHARLES C. LITTLE AND JAMES BROWN, / 1846.

Pagination: [1-3] 4-43 [44].

Collation: [1]^4 2-5^4 6^2.

Contents: p. 1: title page; p. 2: printer's imprint; pp. 3-43: text;
p. 44: blank.

Typography and paper: page size: 9 3/4" X 6 1/16"; text size:
6 3/16" X 3 5/8"; wove paper; 32 lines per page. No running heads.

Binding: light gray; light tan wrappers: front recto: all within a
triple-rule frame with ornamental corners: the same as the title
page, except: 'A . . . JAMES BROWN. / [rule] / PRINTED BY I. R.
BUTTS. / 1846.'; front verso and back recto and verso: blank. All
edges trimmed.

Printing: I. R. Butts, Boston.

Publication: Unknown.

Locations: JM, MH.

A 12.2

Presumed second edition, only printing (1846)

Title page: The same as the first edition, except: 'A . . .
REQUEST. / [rule] / THIRD EDITION. / [rule] / BOSTON: / PRINTED BY
I. R. BUTTS. / [rule] / 1846.'.

33pp. Cover title. *Locations:* DLC, JM, MH, MH-AH.

Note: No second edition has been located.

A 13   A SERMON OF THE PERISHING CLASSES IN BOSTON
          1846

A 13.1.a

First edition, first printing (1846)

A / SERMON / OF THE / PERISHING CLASSES IN BOSTON; / PREACHED AT / THE MELODEON, / ON / SUNDAY, AUGUST 30, 1846. / BY / THEODORE PARKER, / MINISTER OF THE TWENTY-EIGHTH CONGREGATIONAL CHURCH IN BOSTON. / [rule] / PUBLISHED BY REQUEST. / [rule] / BOSTON: / PRINTED BY I. R. BUTTS, / [rule] / 1846.

Pagination: [1–3] 4–28.

Collation: [1]^6 2^6 3^2.

Contents: p. 1: title page; p. 2: blank; pp. 3–28: text.

Typography and paper: page size: 8" X 4 7/8"; text size: 5 5/8" (5 5/16") X 3 1/4"; wove paper; 40 lines per page. Running heads: rectos: pp. 5–27: 'PERISHING CLASSES IN BOSTON.'; versos: pp. 4–26: 'SERMON ON THE'; p. 28: 'SERMON OF THE PERISHING CLASSES IN BOSTON.'.

Binding: Cover title. Untrimmed.

Printing: I. R. Butts. Boston.

Publication: Unknown.

Locations: BL, JM, MBAt, MH, MH-AH, NcD.

A 13.1.b

First edition, second printing (1847)

Title page: The same as in the first printing, except: 'A . . .
REQUEST. / [rule] / SECOND EDITION. / [rule] / BOSTON: / PUBLISHED
BY BENJAMIN H. GREENE. / Printed, and sold, by I. R. Butts, No. 2
School Street. / [rule] / 1847.'.

28pp. Cover title. *Locations:* JM, MH, MH-AH.

36

A 14   A SERMON OF IMMORTAL LIFE
         1846

A 14.1

First edition, only printing (1846)

A / SERMON / OF / IMMORTAL LIFE: / PREACHED AT THE / MELODEON, /
[gothic] On Sunday September 20th, 1846, / BY / THEODORE PARKER, /
MINISTER OF THE XXVIII. CONGREGATIONAL CHURCH IN BOSTON, / AND NOW /
PUBLISHED BY REQUEST. / BOSTON: / PRINTED BY GEORGE COOLIDGE, / No.
1½ Water Street. / 1846.

Pagination: [1–3] 4–32.

Collation: [1]^4 2–4^4.

Contents: p. 1: title page; p. 2: copyright information; pp. 3–32:
text.

Typography and paper: page size: 9 5/16" X 5 3/4"; text size: 6 5/8"
X 3 9/16"; wove paper; 34 lines per page. No running heads.

Binding: light gray; light tan wrappers: front recto: all within a
triple-rule frame: the same as the title page, except: 'A . . .
BOSTON: / JORDAN & WILEY, / No. 20 State Street. / 1846.'; front
verso and back recto and verso: blank. All edges trimmed.

Printing: George Coolidge, 1 1/2 Water Street, Boston.

Publication: Deposited for copyright: title, 10 March 1847.

Locations: BL, JM, MH, MH-AH.

A 14.2

Second edition, only printing (1850)

Title page: A / SERMON / OF / IMMORTAL LIFE: / PREACHED AT THE
MELODEON. / On Sunday, September 20th, 1846, / BY THEODORE PARKER, /
MINISTER OF THE XXVIII. CONGREGATIONAL CHURCH IN BOSTON. / AND NOW
PUBLISHED BY REQUEST. / [gothic] Second Edition. / BOSTON: / WM.
CROSBY AND H. P. NICHOLS. / 111 WASHINGTON STREET. / 1850.

29pp. Wrappers. Price, 10¢. *Locations:* MCo, MH.

A 14.3.a

Presumed third edition, first printing (1855)

Title page: A / SERMON / OF / IMMORTAL LIFE: / PREACHED AT THE
MELODEON, / On Sunday, September 20th, 1846. / BY THEODORE PARKER, /
MINISTER OF THE XXVIII. CONGREGATIONAL CHURCH IN BOSTON. / AND NOW
PUBLISHED BY REQUEST. / [gothic] Fourth Edition. / BOSTON: /
PUBLISHED BY BELA MARSH, / No. 15 Franklin Street. / 1855.

30pp. Wrappers. Price, 10¢. *Location:* NN.

Note: No third edition has been located.

A 14.3.b

Presumed third edition, second printing (1858)

Title page: The same as in the presumed third edition, first
printing, except: 'A . . . REQUEST. / [gothic] Fifth Edition. /
BOSTON: / PUBLISHED BY BELA MARSH, / 14 BROMFIELD STREET. / 1858.'.

30pp. Wrappers. Price, 10¢. *Location:* MH.

A 14.3.c

Presumed third edition, third printing (1870)

Title page: The same as in the presumed third edition, first
printing, except: 'A . . . REQUEST. / [gothic] New Edition. /
BOSTON: / HORACE B. FULLER, / 14 BROMFIELD STREET. / 1870.'.

30pp. + 2pp. on Parker and the Boston Music Hall by George William
Curtis. Wrappers. Price, 15¢. *Location:* JM.

A 14.4.a-q

Fourth edition, first through seventeenth printings [1902?-1930]

Title page: A SERMON ON IMMORTAL LIFE / THEODORE PARKER / [two lines
in lower left] Series Ten / Number Three

25pp. Cover title. Published by the American Unitarian
Association, Boston. *Locations:* DLC, MH, MH-AH. Also reprinted
(first printing, November 1906) in *Memorable Sermons*, no. 3, with
the following cover title: '[rule] / [rule] / A Sermon on Immortal
Life / THEODORE PARKER / [MEMORABLE SERMONS, NO. 3] / PUBLISHED
FOR FREE DISTRIBUTION / AMERICAN UNITARIAN ASSOCIATION / 25 BEACON
STREET, BOSTON / [rule] / [rule]'. *Locations:* JM (17th printing,
April 1930), MH-AH (n.d.).

A 15   A SERMON OF MERCHANTS
         1847

A 15

First edition, only printing (1847)

A / SERMON OF MERCHANTS: / PREACHED AT THE / MELODEON, / ON SUNDAY,
NOVEMBER 22d, 1846. / BY / THEODORE PARKER, / MINISTER OF THE
XXVIII. CONGREGATIONAL CHURCH IN BOSTON. / PUBLISHED BY REQUEST. /
BOSTON: / PRINTED BY GEORGE COOLIDGE, / No. 1½ Water Street. / 1847.

Pagination: [1–3] 4–47 [48].

Collation: [1]^4 2-6^4.

Contents: p. 1: title page; p. 2: copyright information; pp. 3–47:
text; p. 48: blank.

Typography and paper: page size: 9 1/16'' X 5 3/4''; text size: 6 5/8''
X 3 9/16''; wove paper; 34 lines per page. No running heads.

Binding: light gray; light tan wrappers: front recto: all within a
triple-rule frame: the same as the title page, except: 'A . . .
BOSTON: / JORDAN & WILEY, / No. 20 State Street. / 1847.'; front
verso and back recto and verso: blank. All edges trimmed.

Printing: George Coolidge, 1 1/2 Water Street, Boston.

Publication: Deposited for copyright: title, 10 March 1847.

Locations: JM, MH, MH-AH, MHi.

A 16   A SERMON OF THE DANGEROUS CLASSES IN SOCIETY
           1847

A 16

First edition, only printing (1847)

A / SERMON / OF / THE DANGEROUS CLASSES IN SOCIETY, / [gothic]
Preached at the Melodeon, on Sunday, Jan. 31, / BY / THEODORE
PARKER, / MINISTER OF THE XXVIII. CONGREGATIONAL CHURCH IN
BOSTON, / AND NOW PUBLISHED BY REQUEST. / BOSTON: / PUBLISHED BY
C. & J. M. SPEAR, 40 CORNHILL, / AND B. H. GREENE, 124 WASHINGTON
STREET. / 1847.

Pagination: [1-3] 4-48.

Collation: [1]^8 2-3^8.

Contents: p. 1: title page; p. 2: copyright information and
printer's imprint; pp. 3-48: text.

Typography and paper: page size: 9 3/16" X 5 13/16"; text size:
6 5/8" X 3 9/16"; wove paper; 34 lines per page. No running heads.

Binding: light gray; light tan wrappers: front recto: all within a
triple-rule frame: the same as the title page; front verso and
back recto and verso: blank. All edges trimmed.

Printing: Coolidge and Wiley, Water Street, Boston.

Publication: Deposited for copyright: title, 28 April 1847; book,
15 June 1847.

Locations: JM, MH, MH-AH, MHi, RPB.

A 17 A LETTER TO THE PEOPLE OF THE UNITED STATES TOUCHING THE
MATTER OF SLAVERY
1848

A 17.1.a

First edition, first printing (1848)

A / LETTER / TO THE / PEOPLE OF THE UNITED STATES / TOUCHING THE /
MATTER OF SLAVERY. / BY / THEODORE PARKER. / [rule] / BOSTON: /
JAMES MUNROE AND COMPANY. / [rule] / MDCCCXLVIII.

Pagination: [1-5] 6-9 [10] 11-27 [28] 29-41 [42] 43-57 [58] 59-78
[79] 80-103 [104] 105-111 [112] 113-120.

Collation: [1]^6 2-10^6.

Contents: p. 1: 'A / LETTER / TO THE / PEOPLE OF THE UNITED
STATES.'; p. 2: blank; p. 3: title page; p. 4: printer's
information; pp. 5-120: text, signed 'THEODORE PARKER. / *Boston,
December* 22, 1847.'.

Typography and paper: page size: 7 5/8" X 4 5/8"; text size: 5 1/4"
(4 15/16") X 3 1/8"; wove paper; 29 lines per page. Running heads:
rectos and versos: 'LETTER ON SLAVERY.'.

Binding: Two styles have been noted, priority undetermined:

> *Binding A:* light gray; light tan wrappers: front recto: all
> within a single-rule frame: the same as the title page,
> except: 'LETTER / TO . . . COMPANY. / 134 WASHINGTON
> STREET. / [rule] / MDCCCXLVIII.'; front verso and back
> recto: blank; back verso: all within a single-rule frame:
> advertisement for eight titles published by James Munroe.
> All edges trimmed.

> *Binding B:* black; medium brown T cloth (rib); front cover:
> blindstamped triple-rule frame with goldstamped 'A / LETTER /

TO THE / PEOPLE OF THE UNITED STATES' in the center; back cover: blindstamped triple-rule frame; spine: blindstamped rules. Flyleaves. Cream coated; yellow coated; pale yellow endpapers. All edges trimmed.

Printing: Freeman and Bolles, Devonshire Street, Boston.

Publication: Listed in the *English Catalogue* under the title *Letter on Slavery in the United States* as an importation by Chapman at 2s6d.

Locations: Binding A: JM, MH-AH; Binding B: BL, JM, MB, MBAt.

A 17.1.b
First edition, second printing (1971)

Title page: A / LETTER / TO THE / PEOPLE OF THE UNITED STATES / BY / THEODORE PARKER / *The Black Heritage Library Collection* / [publisher's logo to the left of the next two lines] BOOKS FOR LIBRARIES PRESS / FREEPORT, NEW YORK / 1971

120pp. Facsimile reprinting. Deposit copy: DLC (21 May 1971). Price, $8.50. *Locations:* DLC, ScU.

A 17.1.c
First edition, third printing (1972)

Title page: The same as in the first printing, except: 'A . . . MDCCCXLVIII. / Reprinted 1972 / Scholarly Press, Inc., 22929 Industrial Drive East / St. Clair Shores, Michigan 48080'.

120pp. Facsimile reprinting. Deposit copy: DLC (20 June 1972). Price, $14.50. *Locations:* DLC, ScU.

A 18   SOME THOUGHTS ON THE MOST CHRISTIAN USE OF THE SUNDAY 1848

A 18.1

First edition, only printing (1848)

SOME THOUGHTS / ON THE / MOST CHRISTIAN USE OF THE SUNDAY: / A SERMON / PREACHED AT THE MELODEON, ON SUNDAY, JAN. 30TH, / BY THEODORE PARKER, / MINISTER OF THE XXVIII. CONGREGATIONAL CHURCH IN BOSTON: / AND NOW PUBLISHED BY REQUEST. / BOSTON: / B. H. GREENE, 124 WASHINGTON STREET. / 1848.

Pagination: [1–3] 4 [5] 6–51 [52].

Collation: $[1]^8 \ 2\text{--}3^8 \ 4^2$.

Contents: p. 1: title page; p. 2: copyright information and printer's imprint; pp. 3–4: 'MORNING LESSON.'; pp. 5–51: text; p. 52: blank.

Typography and paper: page size: 9 3/8'' X 5 3/4''; text size: 6 1/8'' X 3 1/2''; wove paper; 'Morning Lesson': various lines per page; text: 31 lines per page. No running heads.

Binding: light gray; light tan wrappers: front recto: all within a triple-rule frame: the same as the title page; front verso and back recto and verso: blank. All edges trimmed.

Printing: Coolidge and Wiley, Corner Water and Devonshire Streets, Boston.

Publication: Deposited for copyright: title, 11 March 1848.

Locations: BL, JM, MBAt, MH, MH–AH.

44

A 18.2

First English edition, only printing (1866)

SOME THOUGHTS / ON THE MOST / CHRISTIAN USE OF THE SUNDAY: / A
SERMON / PREACHED AT THE MELODEON, IN BOSTON, MASSACHUSETTS, / ON
SUNDAY, JANUARY 30, 1848. / BY / THEODORE PARKER, / MINISTER OF THE
28TH CONGREGATIONAL CHURCH IN BOSTON. / [rule] / EDINBURGH: /
EDMONSTON & DOUGLAS. / LONDON: HAMILTON, ADAMS, & CO.   GLASGOW:
J. MACLEHOSE. / [rule] / MDCCCLXVI.

Pagination: [1–3] 4–28 [29] 30–31 [32].

Collation: [A]^8 B^8.

Contents: p. 1: title page; p. 2: unsigned editorial note; pp.
3–28: text; pp. 29–31: 'NOTES BY THE EDITOR.'; p. 32: publishers'
advertisement.

Typography and paper: page size: 9 1/4" X 5 1/2"; text size: 7"
(6 3/4") X 3 13/16"; wove paper; 41 lines per page. Running heads:
rectos: pp. 5–27: 'CHRISTIAN USE OF THE SUNDAY.'; p. 31: 'NOTES.';
versos: pp. 4–26: 'THOUGHTS ON THE MOST'; p. 28: 'THOUGHTS ON THE
MOST CHRISTIAN USE OF SUNDAY.'; p. 30: 'NOTES.'.

Binding: Cover title. All edges trimmed.

Printing: Neill and Company, Edinburgh.

Publication: Deposit copy: BL (30 March 1866).

Locations: BE, BL.

A 19   A DISCOURSE OCCASIONED BY THE DEATH OF JOHN QUINCY ADAMS
1848

A 19

First edition, only printing (1848)

A / DISCOURSE / OCCASIONED BY THE / DEATH OF / JOHN QUINCY ADAMS: /
DELIVERED AT THE MELODEON IN BOSTON, MARCH 5, 1848. / [rule] / BY
THEODORE PARKER, / MINISTER OF THE TWENTY-EIGHTH CONGREGATIONAL
CHURCH IN BOSTON. / [rule] / BOSTON: / PUBLISHED BY BELA MARSH, 25
CORNHILL. / 1848.

Pagination: [1-3] 4-66 [67-68].

Collation: [1]^8 2-4^8 [5]^2.

Contents: p. 1: title page; p. 2: 'REPRINTED FROM THE MASSACHUSETTS
QUARTERLY REVIEW.' and printer's imprint; pp. 3-66: text; pp. 67-68:
blank.

Typography and paper: page size: 9 3/8" X 5 7/8"; text size:
6 1/16" X 3 1/2"; wove paper; 30 lines per page. No running heads.

Binding: light gray; light tan wrappers: front recto: all within a
triple-rule frame: the same as the title page; front verso and back
recto and verso: blank. All edges trimmed.

Printing: Coolidge and Wiley, Corner Water and Devonshire Streets,
Boston.

Publication: For evidence that the discourse was published by 14
March 1848, see Weiss, *Life and Correspondence* (C 5), 1:300.
Inscribed copy: MBAt (from Parker, 5 June 1848).

Locations: JM, MBAt, MH, MH-AH.

Note: First printed in the *Massachusetts Quarterly Review*, 1 (June
1848): 331-375.

A 20   A SERMON OF THE MEXICAN WAR
         1848

A 20

First edition, only printing (1848)

A SERMON / OF THE / MEXICAN WAR: / PREACHED AT THE MELODEON, ON
SUNDAY, JUNE 25TH, 1848, / BY THEODORE PARKER, / MINISTER OF THE
XXVIII. CONGREGATIONAL CHURCH IN BOSTON. / PUBLISHED BY REQUEST. /
BOSTON: / COOLIDGE AND WILEY, 12 WATER STREET. / 1848.

Pagination: [1–3] 4 [5] 6–56.

Collation: [1]^8 2–3^8 4^4.

Contents: p. 1: title page; p. 2: copyright information; pp. 3–4:
'SCRIPTURE LESSON.'; pp. 5–56: text.

Typography and paper: page size: 9" X 5 3/4"; text size: 6 3/8" X
3 1/2"; wove paper; 33 lines per page. No running heads.

Binding: light tan wrappers: front recto: all within a triple–rule
frame: the same as the title page; front verso and back recto and
verso: blank. All edges trimmed.

Printing: Coolidge and Wiley, Boston.

Publication: Deposited for copyright: title, 10 August 1848.

Location: JM.

Note: First printed in the *Massachusetts Quarterly Review*, 1
(December 1847): 8–53.

A 21   A SERMON OF THE MORAL CONDITION OF BOSTON AND A SERMON OF
       THE SPIRITUAL CONDITION OF BOSTON
       1849

A 21

First edition, only printing (1849)

Two title pages are present:

A / SERMON / OF THE / MORAL CONDITION OF BOSTON, / PREACHED AT THE
MELODEON, ON SUNDAY, FEB. 11, 1849, / BY THEODORE PARKER, /
MINISTER OF THE XXVIII. CONGREGATIONAL CHURCH. / PUBLISHED BY
REQUEST. / BOSTON: / PUBLISHED BY CROSBY AND NICHOLS, / 111
WASHINGTON STREET. / 1849.

and

A / SERMON / OF THE / SPIRITUAL CONDITION OF BOSTON, / PREACHED AT
THE MELODEON, ON SUNDAY, FEB. 18, 1849, / BY THEODORE PARKER, /
MINISTER OF THE XXVIII. CONGREGATIONAL CHURCH. / PUBLISHED BY
REQUEST. / BOSTON: / PUBLISHED BY CROSBY AND NICHOLS, / 111
WASHINGTON STREET. / 1849.

Pagination: [1-3] 4-36 [37-39] 40-74 [75-76].

Collation: [1]^6 2-3^6 [4]^6 5-6^6 7^2.

Contents: p. 1: first title page; p. 2: printer's imprint; pp.
3-36: text of "A Sermon of the Moral Condition of Boston"; p. 37:
second title page; p. 38: blank; pp. 39-74: text of "A Sermon of
the Spiritual Condition of Boston"; pp. 75-76: blank.

Typography and paper: page size: 8" X 4 7/8"; text size: 5 13/16"
X 3 1/4"; wove paper; 40 lines per page. No running heads.

Binding: Two styles have been noted, priority undetermined:

Binding A: Cover title (first title page). All edges trimmed.

Binding B: light gray; light tan wrappers: front recto: '[rule] / [rule] / MR. PARKER'S SERMONS / OF THE / MORAL AND SPIRITUAL CONDITION / OF / BOSTON. / [rule] / [rule]'; front verso and back recto and verso: blank. All edges trimmed.

Printing: Coolidge and Wiley, Water Street, Boston.

Publication: Unknown.

Locations: Binding A: MH-AH; Binding B: JM, MBAt, MHi, ViU.

A 22   THE PUBLIC EDUCATION OF THE PEOPLE
1850

A 22

First edition, only printing (1850)

[gothic] The Public Education of the People. / [rule] / AN /
ORATION / DELIVERED BEFORE / THE ONONDAGA TEACHERS' INSTITUTE, /
AT SYRACUSE, N.Y., / On the 4th of October, 1849. / BY THEODORE
PARKER. / PUBLISHED BY REQUEST. / BOSTON: / WM. CROSBY & H. P.
NICHOLS, / 111 WASHINGTON STREET. / 1850.

Pagination: [1-3] 4-59 [60].

Collation: [1]^4 2-7^4 8^2.

Contents: p. 1: title page; p. 2: copyright information and
printer's imprint; pp. 3-59: text; p. 60: blank.

Typography and paper: page size: 9 1/2" X 5 5/8"; text size:
6 1/16" X 3 9/16"; wove paper; 31 lines per page. No running heads.

Binding: Two styles have been noted, priority undetermined:

> *Binding A:* Cover title. All edges trimmed.

> *Binding B:* light gray wrappers: front recto: all within a
> triple-rule frame: the same as the title page; front verso
> and back recto and verso: blank. All edges trimmed.

Printing: Coolidge and Wiley, 12 Water Street, Boston.

Publication: Unknown.

Locations: Binding A: JM; Binding B: MH-AH.

A 23   THEODORE PARKER'S REVIEW OF WEBSTER
         1850

A 23.1

Presumed first edition, only printing (1850)

[gothic] Theodore Parker's Review of Webster. / [rule] / SPEECH /
OF / THEODORE PARKER, / DELIVERED IN / THE OLD CRADLE OF LIBERTY, /
MARCH 25, 1850. / [ornate rule] / BOSTON: / R. F. WALLCUT, 21
CORNHILL. / 1850.

Pagination: [1–3] 4–26.

Collation: [a]^1 1–2^6.

Contents: p. 1: title page; p. 2: blank; pp. 3–26: text.

Typography and paper: page size: 8 7/8" X 5 9/16"; text size:
6 9/16" (6 5/16") X 3 1/2"; wove paper; 36 lines per page. Running
heads: rectos: pp. 5–25: 'THEODORE PARKER.'; versos: pp. 4–24:
'SPEECH OF'; p. 26: 'SPEECH OF THEODORE PARKER.'.

Binding: light tan wrappers: front recto: all within a triple-rule
frame: the same as the title page; front verso and back recto and
verso: blank. All edges trimmed.

Printing: Unknown.

Publication: Inscribed copies: MH (lacks back wrapper; from Parker,
22 July 1850); MBAt (lacks back wrapper; from Parker, 1 November
1850).

Locations: JM, MH–AH.

Review of Webster's Speech.

BY THEODORE PARKER.

52

A 23.2

Presumed second edition, only printing [1850?]

[bold lettering] Review of Webster's Speech. / BY THEODORE PARKER. / [rule] / [rule] / [four columns of text separated by single rules]

Broadside, printed on both sides. *See illustration on p. 51.*

Typography and paper: page size: 20" X 14"; text size: 18" X 10 1/2"; newsprint; 118 lines per column on front; 130 lines per column on back. No running heads.

Printing: Unknown.

Publication: Unknown.

Locations: BL, DLC, MH.

A 24   THE FUNCTION AND PLACE OF CONSCIENCE
1850

A 24

First edition, only printing (1850)

THE / FUNCTION AND PLACE OF CONSCIENCE, / IN RELATION TO THE LAWS
OF MEN; / A SERMON FOR THE TIMES; / PREACHED AT THE MELODEON, ON
SUNDAY, SEPTEMBER 22, 1850. / BY / THEODORE PARKER, / MINISTER OF
THE XXVIII. CONGREGATIONAL CHURCH IN BOSTON. / PUBLISHED BY
REQUEST. / BOSTON: / CROSBY & NICHOLS, / 1850.

Pagination: [1–3] 4–5 [6–7] 8–40.

Collation: [1]^8 2^8 3^4.

Contents: p. 1: title page; p. 2: blank; pp. 3–5: 'SCRIPTURE
LESSON.'; p. 6: blank; pp. 7–40: text.

Typography and paper: page size: 9" X 5 9/16"; text size: 6 9/16"
X 3 5/8"; wove paper; "Scripture Lesson": 61 lines per page; text:
34 lines per page. No running heads.

Binding: light gray; light tan wrappers: front recto: all within a
triple-rule frame: '[ornate rule] / MR. PARKER'S SERMON OF
CONSCIENCE / [ornate rule]'; front verso and back recto and verso:
blank. All edges trimmed.

Printing: Unknown.

Publication: Unknown.

Locations: BL, JM, MH, MH-AH.

A 25   THE STATE OF THE NATION
         1851

A 25

First edition, only printing (1851)

THE / STATE OF THE NATION, / CONSIDERED IN / A SERMON FOR
THANKSGIVING DAY, / PREACHED AT THE MELODEON, NOV. 28, 1850. / BY /
THEODORE PARKER, / Minister of the xxviii. Congregational Society
in Boston. / *(REPRINTED FROM THE PHONOGRAPHIC REPORT OF THE
CHRONOTYPE.)* / BOSTON: / WM. CROSBY AND H. P. NICHOLS. / M DCCC LI.

Pagination: [1–3] 4–38 [39–40].

Collation: [1]^4 2–5^4.

Contents: p. 1: title page; p. 2: printer's imprint; pp. 3–38:
text; pp. 39–40: blank.

Typography and paper: page size: 9 1/4" X 5 11/16"; text size:
6 1/2" X 3 5/8"; wove paper; 36 lines per page. No running heads.

Binding: light tan wrappers: front recto: all within a double–rule
frame: '[rule] / MR. PARKER'S SERMON / ON THE / STATE OF THE
NATION. / [rule]'; front verso and back recto and verso: blank.
All edges trimmed.

Printing: Thurston, Torrey, and Emerson, Devonshire Street, Boston.

Publication: Unknown.

Location: JM.

A 26   THE CHIEF SINS OF THE PEOPLE
          1851

A 26

First edition, only printing (1851)

[gothic] The Chief Sins of the People: / A / SERMON / DELIVERED AT
THE MELODEON, BOSTON, / ON FAST-DAY, APRIL 10, 1851. / BY REV.
THEODORE PARKER. / [rule] / PHONOGRAPHICALLY REPORTED BY ROBERT
BOND. / [rule] / BOSTON: / BENJAMIN H. GREENE, / 124, WASHINGTON
STREET. / 1851.

Pagination: [1-3] 4-40.

Collation: [1]^4 2-5^4.

Contents: p. 1: title page; p. 2: printer's imprint; pp. 3-40: text.

Typography and paper: page size: 9 7/16" X 5 13/16"; text size:
6 1/2" X 3 5/8"; wove paper; 38 lines per page. No running heads.

Binding: light gray; light tan wrappers: front recto: all within a
triple-rule frame: the same as the title page; front verso and back
recto and verso: blank. All edges trimmed.

Printing: John Wilson and Son, 22 School Street, Boston.

Publication: Unknown.

Locations: MH, MH-AH, MHi, RPB.

CAUTION!!

COLORED PEOPLE

OF BOSTON, ONE & ALL,

You are hereby respectfully **CAUTIONED** and advised, to avoid conversing with the

Watchmen and Police Officers of Boston,

For since the recent **ORDER OF THE MAYOR & ALDERMEN,** they are empowered to act as

KIDNAPPERS

AND

Slave Catchers,

And they have already been actually employed in **KIDNAPPING, CATCHING, AND KEEPING SLAVES.** Therefore, if you value your **LIBERTY,** and the *Welfare of the Fugitives* among you, *Shun* them in every possible manner, as so many *HOUNDS* on the track of the most unfortunate of your race.

Keep a Sharp Look Out for KIDNAPPERS, and have TOP EYE open.

APRIL 24, 1851.

A 27

A 27   CAUTION!! COLORED PEOPLE OF BOSTON
1851

A 27

First edition, only printing (1851)

[See illustration on p. 56]

Broadside, printed on recto only.

Typography and paper: page size: 15 7/8" X 10 5/8"; text size: 13 7/8" X 9"; wove paper; 23 lines. No running head.

Printing: Unknown.

Publication: Unknown.

Location: MB.

Note one: For Parker's authorship, see his letter to F. Jackson, 20 April 1851 (MB).

Note two: Parker may have written similar abolitionist broadsides: see Weiss, *Life and Correspondence* (C 5), 2:132–135, and various broadsides, formerly in a scrapbook assembled by Parker's wife, at MB.

58

A 28   THE THREE CHIEF SAFEGUARDS OF SOCIETY
        1851

A 28
First edition, only printing (1851)

THE / THREE / CHIEF SAFEGUARDS OF SOCIETY, / CONSIDERED IN / A
SERMON / AT / THE MELODEON, ON SUNDAY, JULY 6, 1851. / BY / THEODORE
PARKER, / MINISTER OF THE TWENTY-EIGHTH CONGREGATIONAL CHURCH IN
BOSTON. / BOSTON: / WM. CROSBY AND H. P. NICHOLS, / 111, WASHINGTON
STREET. / 1851.

Pagination: [1-3] 4-40.

Collation: [1]^4 2-5^4.

Contents: p. 1: title page; p. 2: printer's imprint; pp. 3-40: text.

Typography and paper: page size: 9 3/16" X 6"; text size: 6 1/2" X
3 11/16"; wove paper; 35 lines per page. No running heads.

Binding: light gray; light tan wrappers; front recto: all within a
triple-rule frame: the same as the title page; front verso and back
recto and verso: blank. All edges trimmed.

Printing: John Wilson and Son, 22 School Street, Boston.

Publication: Inscribed copy: MH (6 October 1851).

Locations: DLC, MH, MH-AH.

A 29   SPEECHES, ADDRESSES, AND OCCASIONAL SERMONS
         1852

A 29.1

First edition, only printing (1852)

SPEECHES, ADDRESSES, / AND / OCCASIONAL SERMONS, / BY / THEODORE
PARKER, / MINISTER OF THE XXVIIIth CONGREGATIONAL CHURCH IN
BOSTON. / IN TWO VOLUMES. / VOL. I. [II.] / BOSTON: / WM. CROSBY
AND H. P. NICHOLS. / NEW YORK: C. S. FRANCIS & COMPANY. /
M DCCC LII.

Pagination: vol. 1: [i–v] vi [1] 2–16 [17] 18–45 [46] 47–80 [81]
82–90 [91] 92–132 [133] 134–162 [163] 164–200 [201] 202–238 [239]
240–260 [261] 262–297 [298] 299–336 [337] 338–371 [372] 373–395
[396] 397–437 [438–439] 440–442 [443–444]; vol. 2: [i–iii] iv [1]
2–39 [40] 41–96 [97] 98–106 [107] 108–118 [119] 120–146 [147]
148–173 [174] 175–208 [209] 210–240 [241] 242–276 [277] 278–312
[313] 314–356 [357] 358–394 [395] 396–440 [441–444].

Collation: vol. 1: [a]^2 [b]^1 1–37^6; vol. 2: [a]^2 1–37^6.

Contents: vol. 1: p. i: title page; p. ii: copyright information
and printer's imprint; p. iii: 'PREFACE.' dated 'August 24, 1851.';
p. iv: blank; pp. v–vi: contents; pp. 1–16: "The Relation of Jesus
to His Age and the Ages"; pp. 17–45: "The Idea of a Christian
Church"; pp. 46–80: "A Sermon of War"; pp. 81–90: "A Speech
Delivered at the Anti-Slavery Meeting in Faneuil Hall, February 4,
1847"; pp. 91–132: "A Sermon of the Mexican War"; pp. 133–162: "A
Sermon of the Perishing Classes"; pp. 163–200: "A Sermon of
Merchants"; pp. 201–238: "A Sermon of the Dangerous Classes in
Society"; pp. 239–260: "A Sermon of Poverty, Preached at the
Melodeon, on Sunday, January 14, 1849"; pp. 261–297: "A Sermon of
the Moral Condition of Boston"; pp. 298–336: "A Sermon of the
Spiritual Condition of Boston"; pp. 337–371: "Some Thoughts on the
Most Christian Use of the Sunday"; pp. 372–395: "A Sermon of
Immortal Life"; pp. 396–437: "The Public Education of the People";

p. 438: blank; pp. 439–442: 'APPENDIX.' with information on Parker's installation in 1845; pp. 443–444: blank; vol. 2: p. i: title page; p. ii: copyright information and printer's imprint; pp. iii–iv: contents; pp. 1–39: "The Political Destination of America, and the Signs of the Times. An Address Delivered Before Several Literary Societies, 1848"; pp. 40–96: "A Discourse Occasioned by the Death of John Quincy Adams"; pp. 97–106: "A Speech at a Meeting of the American Anti-Slavery Society, to Celebrate the Abolition of Slavery by the French Republic, April 6, 1848"; pp. 107–118: "A Speech at Faneuil Hall, Before the New England Anti-Slavery Convention, May 31, 1848"; pp. 119–146: "Some Thoughts on the Free Soil Party, and the Election of General Taylor, December, 1848"; pp. 147–173: "Theodore Parker's Review of Webster"; pp. 174–208: "A Speech at the New England Anti-Slavery Convention in Boston, May 29, 1850"; pp. 209–240: "A Discourse Occasioned by the Death of the Late President Taylor, Preached at the Melodeon, on Sunday, July 14, 1850"; pp. 241–276: "The Function and Place of Conscience, in Relation to the Laws of Men"; pp. 277–312: "The State of the Nation"; pp. 313–356: "The Chief Sins of the People"; pp. 357–394: "The Three Chief Safeguards of Society"; pp. 395–440: "The Position and Duties of the American Scholar. An Address Delivered at Waterville, August 8, 1849"; p. 441: advertisements for five of Parker's works; pp. 442–444: blank.

Typography and paper: page size: 7 11/16" X 4 3/4"; text size: 6 1/16" (5 13/16") X 3 1/4"; wove paper; 36 lines per page. Running heads: vol. 1: rectos: pp. 3–437: chapter titles; p. 441: 'APPENDIX.'; versos: p. vi: 'CONTENTS.'; pp. 2–436: chapter titles; pp. 440–442: 'APPENDIX.'; vol. 2: rectos: pp. 3–439: chapter titles; versos: p. iv: 'CONTENTS.'; pp. 2–440: chapter titles.

Binding: black; medium brown T cloth (rib); front and back covers: blindstamped triple-rule frame with lines connecting the corners of the second and third frames, outside of a single-rule frame with intersecting lines in the corners, with a 4 1/8" oval ornament in the center; spine: blindstamped designs and goldstamped lettering: '[leaf-and-vine design] / SPEECHES, ADDRESSES / AND / OCCASIONAL /

SERMONS / [goldstamped rule] / THEO. PARKER / [floret design] /
[within heraldic-like single-rule frame] VOL. I. [II.] / CROSBY &
NICHOLS / [rules-and-floret design]'. Flyleaves in both volumes.
Pale yellow endpapers. All edges trimmed.

Printing: Thurston, Torrey, and Emerson, Boston.

Publication: Inscribed copy: MH (from Parker, 14 December 1851).
Deposit copy: BL (4 January 1853). Listed in the *English Catalogue*
as an importation at 16s the set. Price, $2.50 the set.

Locations: BL, JM, MH, ScU.

Printing histories: "The Relation of Jesus to His Age and the Ages,"
see A 8; "The Idea of a Christian Church," see A 11; "A Sermon of
War," see A 12; "A Speech Delivered at the Anti-Slavery Meeting in
Faneuil Hall, February 4, 1847," *Liberator*, 17 (19 February 1847):
30-31; "A Sermon of the Mexican War," see A 20; "A Sermon of the
Perishing Classes," see A 13; "A Sermon of Merchants," see A 15;
"A Sermon of the Dangerous Classes in Society," see A 16; "A Sermon
of Poverty, Preached at the Melodeon, on Sunday, January 14, 1849,"
Boston Daily Chronotype, 26 January 1849; "A Sermon of the Moral
Condition of Boston," see A 21; "A Sermon of the Spiritual Condition
of Boston," see A 21; "Some Thoughts on the Most Christian Use of
the Sunday," see A 18; "A Sermon of Immortal Life," see A 14; "The
Public Education of the People," see A 22; "The Political
Destination of America, and the Signs of the Times. An Address
Delivered Before Several Literary Societies, 1848," *Massachusetts
Quarterly Review*, 2 (December 1848): 1-31; "A Discourse Occasioned
by the Death of John Quincy Adams," see A 19; "A Speech at a Meeting
of the American Anti-Slavery Society, to Celebrate the Abolition of
Slavery by the French Republic, April 6, 1848," see *Liberator*, 18
(14 April 1848): 58; "A Speech at Faneuil Hall, Before the New
England Anti-Slavery Convention, May 31, 1848," see *Liberator*, 18
(16 June 1848): 94; "Some Thoughts on the Free Soil Party, and the
Election of General Taylor, December, 1848," *Massachusetts Quarterly
Review*, 2 (December 1848): 105-126; "Theodore Parker's Review of

Webster," see A 23; "A Speech at the New England Anti-Slavery
Convention in Boston, May 29, 1850," *Liberator*, 20 (5 July 1850):
105-106; "A Discourse Occasioned by the Death of the Late President
Taylor, Preached at the Melodeon, on Sunday, July 14, 1850," first
appearance; "The Function and Place of Conscience, in Relation to
the Laws of Men," see A 24; "The State of the Nation," see A 25;
"The Chief Sins of the People," see A 26; "The Three Chief
Safeguards of Society," see A 28; "The Position and Duties of the
American Scholar. An Address Delivered at Waterville, August 8,
1849," first appearance.

A 29.2.a
Second edition, first printing (1860)

Two issues have been noted

A 29.2.a$_1$
First issue (1860)

Title page: SPEECHES, ADDRESSES, / AND / OCCASIONAL SERMONS, / BY /
THEODORE PARKER, / MINISTER OF THE TWENTY-EIGHTH CONGREGATIONAL
CHURCH IN BOSTON. / IN THREE VOLUMES. / VOL. I. [II.] [III.] /
BOSTON: / RUFUS LEIGHTON, JR. / M DCCC LX.

420pp., 398pp., 410pp. *Location:* RPB.

A 29.2.a$_2$
Second issue (1861)

Title page: The same as in the second edition, first printing, first
issue, except: 'SPEECHES . . . BOSTON: / TICKNOR AND FIELDS. /
M DCCC LXI.'.

420pp., 398pp., 410pp. The title leaf is a cancel. *Location:* CtY.

A 29.2.b

Second edition, second printing (1864)

Title page: The same as in the second edition, first printing, first issue, except: 'SPEECHES . . . [III.] / NEW YORK: / PUBLISHED BY D. APPLETON & CO. / BOSTON: T. O. H. P. BURNHAM. / 1864.'.

420pp., 398pp., 410pp. Noted in *[Theodore Parker's Works]* binding (see B 2). Price, $1.50. *Location:* JM.

A 29.2.c

Second edition, third printing (1867)

Title page: The same as in the second edition, first printing, first issue, except: 'SPEECHES . . . BOSTON: / HORACE B. FULLER, / (SUCCESSOR TO WALKER, FULLER, AND COMPANY,) / 245, WASHINGTON STREET. / 1867.'.

420pp., 398pp., 410pp. Noted in *[Theodore Parker's Works]* binding (see B 2). *Location:* JM.

A 29.2.d

Second edition, fourth printing (1871)

Title page: The same as in the second edition, third printing, except: 'SPEECHES . . . FULLER, / 14 BROMFIELD STREET. / 1871.'.

420pp., 398pp., 410pp. Noted in *[Theodore Parker's Works]* binding (see B 2). *Locations:* MH, MH-AH, ViU.

64

A 30   THE BOSTON KIDNAPPING
        1852

A 30.1.a

First edition, first printing (1852)

THE BOSTON KIDNAPPING: / A / DISCOURSE / TO COMMEMORATE / THE
RENDITION OF THOMAS SIMMS, / DELIVERED ON THE FIRST ANNIVERSARY
THEREOF, / APRIL 12, 1852, / BEFORE THE COMMITTEE OF VIGILANCE, /
AT THE MELODEON IN BOSTON. / BY THEODORE PARKER. / [rule] /
BOSTON: / CROSBY, NICHOLS, & COMPANY, / 111, WASHINGTON STREET. /
1852.

Pagination: [1–3] 4–72.

Collation: [1]^4 2-9^4.

Contents: p. 1: title page; p. 2: printer's imprint and letter from
the Committee of Arrangements, dated 16 April 1852, asking to print
Parker's discourse; pp. 3–65: text; pp. 66–68: order of services;
pp. 69–72: letters from T. D. Weld, C. M. Clay, and J. R. Giddings.

Typography and paper: page size: 9 1/16" X 5 5/8"; text size:
6 7/16" X 3 11/16"; wove paper; 35 lines per page. No running
heads.

Binding: Two styles have been noted, priority undetermined:

> *Binding A:* light tan wrapper; front recto: all within a
> single-rule frame: the same as the title page; front verso
> and back recto and verso: blank. All edges trimmed.

> *Binding B:* The same as Binding A, except: triple-rule frame
> on front recto; back recto and verso: unknown.

Printing: John Wilson and Son, 22 School Street, Boston.

Publication: Unknown.

Locations: Binding A: CtY; Binding B: DLC (bound and lacks back wrapper).

Note: A copy has been noted with a bookseller's label pasted under the date on the front wrapper: all within a single-rule frame: '*C. S. FRANCIS & CO.* / BOOKSELLERS, / 252 Broadway, / *New York.*' (CtY).

A 30.1.b
First edition, second printing (1969)

Title page: [engraving of a slave in chains] / [rule] / THE BOSTON KIDNAPPING / *Theodore Parker* / [publisher's logo] / ARNO PRESS / & / THE NEW YORK TIMES / NEW YORK   1969

72pp. Facsimile reprinting. Deposit copy: DLC (21 July 1970). Price, $4.50. *Location:* DLC.

A 31   THE LIFE OF WEBSTER
        1852

A 31.1
First edition, only printing (1852)

THE / LIFE OF WEBSTER. / A SERMON, / PREACHED AT THE MELODEON, IN
BOSTON, / *On Sunday Morning, Oct.* 31, 1852. / [rule] / BY REV.
THEODORE PARKER. / [rule] / ROCHESTER: / PRINTED AT THE BOOK & JOB
OFFICE, 41 MAIN-STREET, / *Opposite the Eagle Bank.* / [rule] / 1852.

Pagination: [1–3] 4–30 [31–32].

Collation: [1–2^8].

Contents: p. 1: title page; p. 2: blank; pp. 3–30: text; pp. 31–32:
blank.

Typography and paper: page size: 8 3/8" X 5 5/16"; text size:
6 5/16" (6 1/8") X 4 1/16"; wove paper; 52 lines per page. Running
heads: rectos and versos: 'LIFE OF WEBSTER.'.

Binding: Cover title. All edges trimmed.

Printing: Book and Job Office, Rochester, New York.

Publication: Unknown.

Location: TxU.

A 31.2

Second edition, only printing (1853)

A / DISCOURSE / OCCASIONED BY THE / DEATH OF DANIEL WEBSTER, / PREACHED AT THE MELODEON / ON SUNDAY, OCTOBER 31, 1852. / [rule] / BY / THEODORE PARKER, / MINISTER OF THE TWENTY-EIGHTH CONGREGATIONAL SOCIETY IN BOSTON. / [rule] / BOSTON: / BENJAMIN B. MUSSEY & CO. / NO. 29, CORNHILL. / 1853.

Pagination: [i–iii] iv [v] vi–vii [viii] 1–108.

Collation: [1]^4 2–14^4 15^2.

Contents: p. i: title page; p. ii: copyright information and printer's imprint; pp. iii–iv: 'PREFACE.' dated 'BOSTON, March 7, 1853.'; pp. v–vii: 'INTRODUCTION.'; p. viii: blank; pp. 1–108: text.

Typography and paper: page size: 9 5/16" X 5 3/4"; text size: 6 1/2" X 3 5/8"; wove paper; "Preface": various lines per page; "Introduction": 34 lines per page; text, 35 lines per page. No running heads.

Binding: Two styles have been noted, priority undetermined:

> *Binding A:* light gray; light tan wrappers: front recto: all within a triple-rule frame: the same as the title page; front verso and back recto and verso: blank. All edges trimmed.

> *Binding B:* medium brown T cloth (rib); front cover: blindstamped triple-rule frame with lines connecting the corners of the second and third frames, outside of a single-rule frame with intersecting lines in the corners, with a 6" oval ornament in the center, with goldstamped 'PARKER'S / DISCOURSE / OF / DANIEL WEBSTER' in the center of the ornament; back cover: the same as the front cover, but without the goldstamped lettering; spine: blank. Back

flyleaf. Yellow endpapers. All edges trimmed.

Printing: John Wilson and Son, School Street, Boston.

Publication: Deposit copy: BL (rebound; 3 August 1853). Prices: cloth, 50¢; wrappers, 38¢.

Locations: Binding A: DLC, JM, MH-AH; Binding B: MB.

A 31.3

Presumed first English edition, only printing [1853]

THE / LIFE / OF / DANIEL WEBSTER. / AN ADDRESS / BY THEODORE
PARKER. / [rule] / LONDON: / WILLIAM TWEEDIE, 337, STRAND. /
[rule] / *Price* 6d.

Pagination: [1–3] 4–46.

Collation: [A1]^1 A2^{12} B2^{10}.

Contents: p. 1: title page; p. 2: printer's imprint; pp. 3–46: text.

Typography and paper: page size: 7 1/16" X 4 1/16"; text size:
5 3/4" (5 9/16") X 3 1/8"; wove paper; 39 lines per page. Running
heads: rectos and versos: 'LIFE OF DANIEL WEBSTER.'.

Binding: gray purplish pink wrappers: front recto: the same as the
title page; front verso: blank; back recto and verso: unknown. All
edges trimmed.

Printing: Woodfall and Kinder, Angel Court, Skinner Street, London.

Publication: Deposit copy: BL (24 January 1853). Inscribed copy:
NN (bound; 1853).

Location: BL (lacks back wrapper).

A 31.4

Presumed second English edition, only printing (1853)

DANIEL WEBSTER; / HIS LIFE, ACTS, AND DEATH. / Being an Address
delivered at the Melodeon, / BOSTON, MASSACHUSETTS, / *On Sunday
Morning, Oct.* 31, 1852, / BY THE / REV. THEODORE PARKER. / [dotted
line] / Extracted from the *"Boston Commonwealth."* / And Recommended
to all Haters of Slavery. / [dotted line] / [gothic] Liverpool, /
SUTTON & HAYWOOD, PARADISE-STREET. / 1853.

Pagination: [1–3] 4–50.

Collation: [A–B]^6 C–D^6 E^1.

Contents: p. 1: title page; p. 2: blank; pp. 3–50: text.

Typography and paper: page size: 7 1/16" X 4 1/4"; text size:
5 5/16" X 3"; wove paper; 30 lines per page. No running heads.

Binding: light tan wrappers: front recto: all within a triple-rule
frame with star designs in each corner: 'DANIEL WEBSTER: / HIS
LIFE, ACTS, AND DEATH.'; front verso, back recto and verso: blank.
All edges trimmed.

Printing: Unknown.

Publication: Unknown.

Location: MB.

A 31.5.a
Presumed third English edition, first printing [1853?]

ORATION / ON THE / DEATH OF DANIEL WEBSTER, / BY THE / REV. THEODORE
PARKER. / [rule] / [28 lines of text]

Pagination: [1] 2–32.

Collation: [1]^4 2-3^4 [4]^4.

Contents: pp. 1–32: text.

Typography and paper: page size: 7 1/4" X 4 13/16"; text size:
6 5/16" X 3 9/16"; wove paper; 48 lines per page. No running heads.

Binding: Head title. All edges trimmed.

Printing: James M'Callum, Spreull's Court, 182 Trongate, Glasgow.

Publication: Published by John Robertson, 21 Maxwell Street, Glasgow.

Location: MWA.

A 31.5.b–c
Presumed third English edition, second and third printings [1853?]

Title page: The same as in the presumed third English edition, first
printing.

32pp. Head title. *Location:* BE (3d thousand).

Note: No copies identified as the second thousand have been located.

72

A 32   TEN SERMONS OF RELIGION
         1853

A 32.1.a

First edition, first printing (1853)

TEN / SERMONS / OF RELIGION, / BY / THEODORE PARKER, / MINISTER OF
THE TWENTY-EIGHTH CONGREGATIONAL CHURCH IN BOSTON. / [rule] /
BOSTON: / CROSBY, NICHOLS, AND COMPANY. / NEW YORK: / CHARLES S.
FRANCIS AND COMPANY. / 1853.

Pagination: [i-v] vi [vii-viii] [1-3] 4-32 [33] 34-65 [66] 67-101
[102] 103-139 [140] 141-186 [187] 188-226 [227] 228-260 [261]
262-313 [314] 315-365 [366] 367-395 [396].

Collation: [a]^4 [1]^6 2-33^6.

Contents: p. i: title page; p. ii: copyright information and
printer's imprint; p. iii: dedication to Ralph Waldo Emerson; p.
iv: blank; pp. v-vi: 'PREFACE.' dated 'August 24th, 1852.'; pp.
vii-viii: contents; p. 1: 'SERMONS.'; p. 2: blank; pp. 3-32: "On
Piety, and the Relation Thereof to Manly Life"; pp. 33-65: "Of
Truth and the Intellect"; pp. 66-101: "Of Justice and the
Conscience"; pp. 102-139: "Of Love and the Affections"; pp. 140-186:
"Of Conscious Religion and the Soul"; pp. 187-226: "Of the Culture
of the Religious Powers"; pp. 227-260: "Of Conscious Religion as a
Source of Strength"; pp. 261-313: "Of Conscious Religion as a Source
of Joy"; pp. 314-365: "Of Conventional and Natural Sacraments"; pp.
366-395: "Of Communion with God"; p. 396: blank.

Typography and paper: page size: 7 7/16" X 4 5/8"; text size:
5 7/16" (5 1/8") X 3 1/4"; wove paper; "Preface": various lines per
page; text: 28 lines per page. Running heads: rectos: pp. 5-395:
titles of selections; versos: p. vi: 'PREFACE.'; pp. 4-394: titles
of selections.

Binding: Two styles have been noted, priority undetermined:

Binding A: medium brown T cloth (rib); front and back covers: blindstamped triple-rule frame with lines connecting the corners of the second and third frames, outside of a single-rule frame with intersecting lines in each corner, with a 4 1/8" oval ornament in the center; spine: blindstamped designs with goldstamped lettering: '[leaf-and-vine design] / PARKER'S / TEN / SERMONS / [leaf-and-vine design] / [oval-like design] / [rules-and-floret design]'. Flyleaves. Pale yellow coated endpapers. All edges trimmed.

Binding B: black T cloth (rib); front and back covers: blindstamped quintuple-rule frame with a leaf design in each corner, with a 4 1/8" oval ornament in the center; spine: blindstamped rules and floral designs with goldstamped 'PARKER'S / TEN / SERMONS'. Flyleaves. Pale yellow endpapers. All edges trimmed.

Printing: Metcalf and Company, Cambridge.

Publication: Deposited for copyright: title, 27 December 1852. Inscribed copies: MB (rebound; from Parker, 1 January 1853); MH-AH (rebound; 8 February 1853); MH (from Parker, 1 July 1853). Price, $1.00.

Locations: Binding A: JM, MH; Binding B: JM.

A 32.1.b
First edition, second printing (1855)

Title page: The same as in the first printing, except: 'TEN . . . CHURCH, IN . . . [rule] / SECOND EDITION. / [rule] / BOSTON: / LITTLE, BROWN AND COMPANY. / 1855.'.

393pp. Deposit copy: BL (7 June 1858). *Locations:* BL, MB, MH, MH-AH, NjP.

A 32.1.c

First edition, third printing (1859)

Two issues have been noted

A 32.1.c$_1$

First issue (1859)

Title page: The same as in the second printing, except: 'TEN . . .
BOSTON: / RUFUS LEIGHTON, JR. / 1859.'.

393pp. Inscribed copy: MH-AH (10 April 1860). Price, $1.00.
Locations: CtY, MH-AH.

A 32.1.c$_2$

Second issue (1861)

Title page: The same as in the second printing, except: 'TEN /
SERMONS OF . . . BOSTON. / SECOND EDITION. / BOSTON: / TICKNOR AND
FIELDS. / M DCCC LXI.'.

393pp. The title leaf is a cancel. Also noted in *[Theodore
Parker's Works]* binding (see B 2); undoubtedly a remainder binding.
Locations: InU, JM (*Works*).

A 32.1.d

First edition, fourth printing (1864)

Title page: The same as in the third printing, second issue,
except: 'TEN . . . EDITION. / NEW YORK: / PUBLISHED BY D. APPLETON
& CO. / BOSTON: T. O. H. P. BURNHAM. / 1864.'.

393pp. Noted in *[Theodore Parker's Works]* binding (see B 2). MBAt
copy received 23 February 1865. Price, $1.50. *Locations:* MB, MBAt.

A 32.2.a

First English edition, first printing (1853)

TEN / SERMONS / OF RELIGION, / BY / THEODORE PARKER, / MINISTER OF THE TWENTY-EIGHTH CONGREGATIONAL CHURCH / IN BOSTON. / [rule] / LONDON: / JOHN CHAPMAN, 142, STRAND. / M DCCC LIII.

Pagination: [i–v] vi [vii–viii] [1–3] 4–30 [31] 32–60 [61] 62–93 [94] 95–127 [128] 129–169 [170] 171–200 [201] 202–249 [250] 251–286 [287] 288–334 [335] 336–361 [362].

Collation: $[A]^4 [B]^{12} C-I^{12} K-Q^{12} [R]^1$.

Contents: p. i: title page; p. ii: blank; p. iii: dedication to Emerson; p. iv: blank; pp. v–vi: 'PREFACE.'; p. vii: contents; p. viii: blank; p. 1: 'SERMONS.'; p. 2: blank; pp. 3–361: text; p. 362: blank.

Typography and paper: page size: 7 3/4" X 4 7/8"; text size: 5 7/16" (5 3/16") X 3"; wove paper; 31 lines per page. Running heads: rectos and versos: chapter titles.

Binding: Unknown.

Printing: Savill and Edwards, Chandos-Street, London.

Publication: Deposit copy: BL (8 February 1853). Price, 8s.

Location: BL (rebound).

Note: Information on pagination, collation, and contents is conjectural since the only located copy has been rebound.

A 32.2.b

First English edition, second printing (1853)

SERMONS / BY / THEODORE PARKER. / [rule] / LONDON: / JOHN CHAPMAN,
142, STRAND. / M DCCC LIII.

Pagination: [i–iv] [1–3]; pp. 4–246 are the same as in the first
printing; [247–248].

Collation: [A]^2 [B]^{12} C–I^{12} K–L^{12} M^4.

Contents: p. i: 'SERMONS.'; p. ii: '⁂ *This Work is Copyright.*';
p. iii: title page; p. iv: blank; pp. 1–246: the same as in the
first printing; pp. 247–248: blank.

Typography and paper: The same as in the first printing; the running
heads end on p. 246.

Binding: dark brown L-like cloth (morocco); front and back covers:
blindstamped quadruple-rule frame, with the second and third frames
intersecting on the sides, outside of a single-rule frame with
ornaments in each corner; spine: blindstamped ornamental rules on
the top and bottom, with goldstamped 'SERMONS / BY / PARKER.'.
Yellow endpapers. All edges trimmed.

Printing: Unknown.

Publication: Deposit copy: BL (20 January 1853). Price, 4s.

Locations: BC, BE, BL, BO.

A 32.3.a

Second English edition, first printing (1863)

Title page: TEN / SERMONS / OF RELIGION. / BY / THEODORE PARKER. /
MINISTER OF THE TWENTY-EIGHTH CONGREGATIONAL CHURCH IN BOSTON. /
LONDON: / TRÜBNER & CO., 60, PATERNOSTER ROW. / 1863.

227pp. + 126pp. "Notice" by Frances Power Cobbe. *Collected Works*,
vol. 2 (see B 1). Deposit copy: BL (19 June 1863). Price, 6s.
Locations: BE, BL, BO, CtY, MH–AH, NcD.

Note: Contains *Ten Sermons of Religion* and *Prayers* (A 63).

A 32.3.b
Second English edition, second printing (1879)

Title page: The same as in the second English edition, first
printing, except: 'TEN . . . CO., LUDGATE HILL. / 1879.'.

227pp. + 126pp. *Collected Works*, vol. 2 (see B 1). *Location:* JM.

78

A 33   TWO SERMONS PREACHED BEFORE THE TWENTY-EIGHTH
        CONGREGATIONAL SOCIETY IN BOSTON
        1853

A 33.1

First edition, only printing (1853)

TWO SERMONS / PREACHED BEFORE THE / TWENTY-EIGHTH CONGREGATIONAL
SOCIETY / IN BOSTON, / ON THE 14TH AND 21ST OF NOVEMBER, 1852, / ON
LEAVING THEIR OLD AND ENTERING A NEW PLACE OF WORSHIP. / BY THEODORE
PARKER, / MINISTER OF THAT SOCIETY. / [rule] / PHONOGRAPHICALLY
REPORTED BY RUFUS LEIGHTON. / [rule] / BOSTON: / CROSBY, NICHOLS,
& COMPANY, / 111, WASHINGTON STREET. / 1853.

Pagination: [1-3] 4-32 [33] 34-56.

Collation: [1]^4 2-7^4.

Contents: p. 1: title page; p. 2: printer's imprint; pp. 3-32: text,
headed 'SERMON I. / [rule] / SOME ACCOUNT OF MY MINISTRY.'; pp.
33-56: text, headed, 'SERMON II. / [rule] / ON THE POSITION AND
DUTY OF A MINISTER.'.

Typography and paper: page size: 9 7/16" X 5 11/16"; text size:
6 1/2" X 3 5/8"; wove paper; 35 lines per page. No running heads.

Binding: light gray; very light tan wrappers: front recto: all
within a triple-rule frame: the same as the title page; front verso
and back recto and verso: blank. All edges trimmed.

Printing: John Wilson and Son, School Street, Boston.

Publication: Price, 20¢.

Locations: JM, MH-AH, MHi.

A 33.2

Second edition, only printing (1853)

Title page: The same as in the first edition, except: 'TWO . . .
BOSTON, / ON THE 14TH AND 21ST OF NOVEMBER, 1852, / ON . . .
LEIGHTON. / [rule] / [gothic] Second Edition. / BOSTON: / BENJAMIN
B. MUSSEY & CO., 29 CORNHILL. / 1853.'.

59pp. Wrappers. *Locations:* JM, MHi.

80

A 34   A SERMON OF THE PUBLIC FUNCTION OF WOMAN
           1853

A 34.1

First edition, only printing (1853)

A / SERMON / OF THE / PUBLIC FUNCTION OF WOMAN, / PREACHED AT THE
MUSIC HALL, MARCH 27, 1853. / BY / THEODORE PARKER, / MINISTER OF
THE TWENTY-EIGHTH CONGREGATIONAL SOCIETY. / [rule] /
PHONOGRAPHICALLY REPORTED BY J. M. W. YERRINTON AND RUFUS
LEIGHTON. / [rule] / BOSTON: / ROBERT F. WALLCUT, 21 CORNHILL. /
1853.

Pagination: [1-5] 6-20.

Collation: $[1]^4 \, 2^6$. Also signed $[1]^4 \, 2^4 \, 3^2$.

Contents: p. 1: title page; p. 2: printer's imprint; p. 3:
'PREFACE.' dated 'BOSTON, APRIL 4, 1853.'; p. 4: blank; pp. 5-20:
text.

Typography and paper: page size: 9 3/16" X 5 5/8"; text size: 6 5/8"
X 3 15/16"; wove paper; 46 lines per page. No running heads.

Binding: light purplish pink; yellow wrappers: front recto: all
within a triple-rule frame with ornaments in each corner: the same
as the title page; front verso and back recto and verso: blank.
All edges trimmed.

Printing: J. B. Yerrinton and Son, 21 Cornhill, Boston.

Publication: Unknown.

Locations: DLC, JM, MH, MH-AH.

A 34.2

Presumed second edition, only printing [1853?]

WOMAN'S RIGHTS TRACTS . . . . . . NO. 2. / [rule] / A SERMON / OF
THE / PUBLIC FUNCTION OF WOMAN, / PREACHED AT THE MUSIC-HALL,
BOSTON / MARCH 27, 1853. / BY THEODORE PARKER. / [rule] / [one line
from Psalm 144:12] / [18 lines of text]

Pagination: [1-2] 3-24.

Collation: [1]^{12}. Signed 2^4 2^8.

Contents: pp. 1-24: text.

Typography and paper: page size: 7 1/8" X 4 5/8"; text size:
5 13/16" (5 1/2") X 3 3/8"; wove paper; 35 lines per page. Running
heads: rectos and versos: 'THE PUBLIC FUNCTION OF WOMAN.'.

Binding: Head title. All edges trimmed.

Printing: Steam Press of Curtis Butts, Rochester, N.Y.

Publication: Woman's Rights Tracts, no. 2.

Locations: JM, MH-AH.

Note one: Also collected in '[all within a double-rule frame]
WOMAN'S RIGHTS / TRACTS. / [rule] / FREEDOM FOR WOMEN, / WENDELL
PHILLIPS. / PUBLIC FUNCTION OF WOMEN, / THEODORE PARKER. /
ENFRANCHISEMENT OF WOMEN, / MRS. JOHN STUART MILLS *[sic]*. / WOMAN
AND HER WISHES, / REV. T. W. HIGGINSON. / RESPONSIBILITIES OF
WOMEN, / MRS. C. I. H. NICHOLS.' with a preface by Lucy Stone.
Wrappers; flexible cloth-covered boards; cloth. Presumably an
early reprinting because the Parker section is signed 2^4 2^8, as is
the original; however, the MBAt copy, presented by Lucy Stone, was
received 17 October 1893. *Locations:* CSt, DLC, MBAt, MH.

Note two: Also collected with the other four tracts in a pamphlet with the following cover title: '[rule] / [rule] / [gothic] Woman's Rights Tracts. / [rule] / [rule]'. Presumably a later reprinting because the Parker section is signed 2^4 [2]^8. *Location:* MWA.

Note three: Also collected with the other four tracts in 'WOMAN'S RIGHTS / TRACTS. / BY WENDELL PHILLIPS, THEODORE PARKER, MRS. / MILL, (OF ENGLAND,) T. W. HIGGINSON, / AND MRS. C. I. H. NICHOLS. / STEREOTYPE EDITION. / [rule] / BOSTON: / ROBERT F. WALLCUT, 21 CORNHILL. / 1854.'. Cloth. The Parker section is signed $1-2^6$. Inscribed copies: all from T. W. Higginson, 4 July 1855: MBAt, MH, MH-AH. *Locations:* MBAt, MH, MH-AH, MWA.

A 34.3.a

First English edition, first printing (1853)

THE / PUBLIC FUNCTION OF WOMAN. / A / SERMON, / PREACHED AT THE MUSIC HALL, MARCH 27, 1853. / BY / THEODORE PARKER, / MINISTER OF THE TWENTY-EIGHTH CONGREGATIONAL SOCIETY. / [rule] / PHONOGRAPHICALLY REPORTED BY J. M. W. YERRINGTON *[sic]* AND RUFUS LEIGHTON. / [rule] / LONDON: / JOHN CHAPMAN, 142, STRAND. / MDCCCLIII.

Pagination: [1-5] 6-23 [24].

Collation: [1]^{12}. Signed [A1]^1 A2^3 A3^8.

Contents: p. 1: title page; p. 2: blank; p. 3: 'PREFACE.'; p. 4: blank; pp. 5-23: text; p. 24: advertisement for three books by Parker.

Typography and paper: page size: 7 9/16" X 4 3/4"; text size: 6 3/16" (5 5/16") X 3 7/16"; wove paper; 45 lines per page. Running heads: rectos and versos: 'THE PUBLIC FUNCTION OF WOMAN'.

Binding: Cover title. All edges trimmed.

Printing: Woodfall and Kinder, Angel Court, Skinner Street, London.

Publication: Deposit copy: BL (2 February 1854).

Locations: BE, BL, BO.

A 34.3.b

First English edition, second printing (1855)

Title page: The same as in the first English edition, first printing, except: 'THE . . . CHAPMAN, 8, KING WILLIAM STREET, STRAND. / MDCCCLV.'.

23pp. Cover title. Price, 6d. *Locations:* CtY, BO.

A 34.4

Fourth edition, only printing [1868]

Title page: A SERMON / OF THE / PUBLIC FUNCTION OF WOMAN, / PREACHED AT THE MUSIC-HALL, BOSTON / MARCH 27, 1853. / BY THEODORE PARKER. / [rule] / [one line from Psalm 144:12] / [18 lines of text]

24pp. Wrappers. Published by the Office of *The Revolution*, New York. Price, 10¢. *Location:* DLC.

A 35   A FRIENDLY LETTER TO THE EXECUTIVE COMMITTEE OF THE
        AMERICAN UNITARIAN ASSOCIATION
        1853

A 35

First edition, only printing (1853)

A / FRIENDLY LETTER / TO THE / EXECUTIVE COMMITTEE / OF THE /
AMERICAN UNITARIAN ASSOCIATION, / TOUCHING / THEIR NEW UNITARIAN
CREED OR GENERAL PROCLAMATION / OF UNITARIAN VIEWS. / [rule] / BY
THEODORE PARKER, / A LIFE MEMBER OF THAT ASSOCIATION, AND MINISTER
OF THE TWENTY-EIGHTH / CONGREGATIONAL CHURCH IN BOSTON. / [rule] /
BOSTON: / BENJAMIN B. MUSSEY & CO. / 1853.

Pagination: [1-3] 4-20.

Collation: [1⁶ 2⁴].

Contents: p. 1: title page; p. 2: blank; pp. 3-20: text.

Typography and paper: page size: 9 1/8" X 5 5/8"; text size: 6 7/16"
X 3 13/16"; wove paper; 34 lines per page. No running heads.

Binding: light gray; light tan wrappers: front recto: all within a
double-rule frame, outside of a single-rule frame with a leaf-and-
vine design in each corner and in the middle of the sides: the same
as the title page, except 'Printed by Bazin & Chandler, 37 Cornhill,
Boston.' is between the second and third frames at the bottom;
front verso and back recto and verso: blank. All edges trimmed.

Printing: Bazin and Chandler, 37 Cornhill, Boston.

Publication: Unknown.

Locations: BL, MHi, MH-AH, NcD, RPB, TxU.

A 36   SERMONS OF THEISM, ATHEISM, AND THE POPULAR THEOLOGY
1853

A 36.1

First edition, only printing (1853)

SERMONS / OF / THEISM, ATHEISM, / AND / THE POPULAR THEOLOGY. /
BY / THEODORE PARKER, / MINISTER OF THE TWENTY-EIGHTH CONGREGATIONAL
SOCIETY / IN BOSTON. / [rule] / BOSTON: / LITTLE, BROWN AND
COMPANY. / 1853.

Pagination: [i–vii] viii [ix] x–lxvi [lxvii–lxviii] [1–3] 4–38 [39]
40–84 [85] 86–127 [128] 129–169 [170] 171–206 [207] 208–247 [248]
249–280 [281] 282–314 [315] 316–362 [363] 364–417 [418–420].

Collation: [A]^6 B–E^6 F^4 [1]^6 2–35^6.

Contents: p. i: title page; p. ii: copyright information and
printer's imprint; p. iii: dedication to William H. White and
George Fiske; p. iv: blank; p. v: 'PREFACE.' dated 'BOSTON, July
16th, 1853.'; p. vi: blank; pp. vii–viii: contents; pp. ix–lxvi:
"Introduction"; pp. lxvii–lxviii: blank; p. 1: 'SERMONS.'; p. 2:
blank; pp. 3–38: "On Speculative Atheism, Regarded as a Theory of
the Universe"; pp. 39–84: "On Practical Theism, Regarded as a
Principle of Ethics"; pp. 85–127: "On the Popular Theology of
Christendom, Regarded as a Theory of the Universe"; pp. 128–169:
"On the Popular Theology of Christendom, Regarded as a Principle of
Ethics"; pp. 170–206: "On Speculative Theism, Regarded as a Theory
of the Universe"; pp. 207–247: "On Practical Theism, Regarded as a
Principle of Ethics"; pp. 248–280: "On the Function and Influence
of the Idea and Influence of Immortal Life"; pp. 281–314: "A Sermon
of Providence"; pp. 315–362: "On the Economy of Pain and Misery
Under the Universal Providence of God"; pp. 363–417: "The Economy
of Moral Error Under the Universal Providence of God"; p. 418:
blank; p. 419: advertisements for eight works by Parker; p. 420:
blank.

Typography and paper: page size: 7 11/16" X 4 3/4"; text size:
"Introduction": 6" (5 3/4") X 3 1/4"; text: 6 11/16" (6 1/2") X
4 1/4"; wove paper; "Introduction": 31 lines per page; text: 28
lines per page. Running heads: rectos: pp. xi–lxv: 'INTRODUCTION.';
pp. 5–417: section titles; versos: p. viii: 'CONTENTS.'; pp. x–lxvi:
'INTRODUCTION.'; pp. 4–416: section titles.

Binding: Two styles have been noted, priority undetermined:

> *Binding A:* light brown L cloth (morocco); front and back
> covers: blindstamped double–rule frame, outside of a
> single–rule frame with loops in each corner and in the
> middle of the sides, with a leaf design inside each corner;
> spine: blindstamped bands with goldstamped 'PARKER'S /
> SERMONS / OF / THEISM'. Flyleaves. Cream; yellow coated
> endpapers. All edges trimmed.

> *Binding B:* black T cloth (rib); front and back covers:
> blindstamped triple–rule frame; spine: the same as Binding
> A. Flyleaves. Pale yellow endpapers. All edges trimmed.

Printing: Allen and Farnham, Remington Street, Cambridge.

Publication: Parker wrote E. Desor on 24 August 1853 that he would
send him a copy "in a few days." On 6 September 1853, Parker
entered into his journal: "This day my new book appeared" (Weiss,
Life and Correspondence [C 5], 1:325, 427). Deposited for
copyright: title, 22 July 1853; book, 6 September 1853. Inscribed
copies: MB (rebound; from Parker, 6 September 1853); MH (from
Parker, 6 September 1853); MH–AH (rebound; 8 September 1853); MH–AH
(lacks spine; from Parker, 13 October 1853). MBAt copy (rebound)
received from Parker 9 September 1854 *[sic?]*.

Locations: Binding A: JM, MH; Binding B: BL.

Note: A copy has been noted with a 21–line errata slip inserted
after p. 420: BL.

A 36.2

First English edition, only printing (1853)

THEISM, ATHEISM, / AND / THE POPULAR THEOLOGY: / SERMONS, / BY / THEODORE PARKER, / AUTHOR OF / "A DISCOURSE OF MATTERS PERTAINING TO RELIGION," / ETC. / LONDON: / JOHN CHAPMAN, 142, STRAND. / MDCCCLIII.

Pagination: [i-ix] x [xi] xii-lx [1] 2-251 [252-255] 256-298 [299-300].

Collation: $[a]^{12}$ b^{12} c^6 B-I^{12} K-N^{12} O^6.

Contents: p. i: '[three lines in gothic] Chapman's / Quarterly Series. / No. I.'; p. ii: blank; inserted leaf with engraving of Parker printed on verso; p. iii: title page; p. iv: printer's imprint; p. v: dedication; p. vi: blank; p. vii: 'PREFACE.'; p. viii: blank; pp. ix-x: contents; pp. xi-lx: 'INTRODUCTION.'; pp. 1-251: text; p. 252: editorial note on the following sermons; p. 253: 'TWO SERMONS / PREACHED BEFORE THE TWENTY EIGHTH CONGREGATIONAL SOCIETY / OF BOSTON, / ON THE 14th & 21st OF NOVEMBER, 1852, / ON LEAVING THEIR OLD AND ENTERING A NEW / PLACE OF WORSHIP. / [rule] / PHONOGRAPHICALLY REPORTED.'; p. 254: blank; pp. 255-279: text of the first sermon; pp. 280-298: text of the second sermon; pp. 299-300: publisher's advertisements.

Typography and paper: page size: 8" X 5"; text size: 6 5/16" (6 1/16") X 3 5/8"; wove paper; 42 lines per page. Running heads: rectos: pp. xiii-lix: 'INTRODUCTION.'; pp. 3-297: topical headings; versos: p. x: 'CONTENTS.'; pp. xii-lx: 'INTRODUCTION.'; pp. 2-298: topical headings.

Binding: dark brown T cloth (rib); dark gray green TR cloth (wavy-grain); front and back covers: blindstamped triple-rule frame with designs in each corner, with a 3" circular "Chapman's Quarterly Series" ornament in the center surrounded by an ornate leaf-and-vine design; spine: blindstamped leaf-and-vine design with goldstamped

'THEISM, ATHEISM, / AND THE / POPULAR THEOLOGY. / [rule] / THEODORE
PARKER. / CHAPMAN'S / QUARTERLY / SERIES. / [rule] / N⁰ 1.'. Yellow
endpapers. All edges trimmed.

Printing: Savill and Edwards, Chandos Street, Covent Garden, London.

Publication: Chapman's Quarterly Series, no. 1. Price, 9s.

Locations: BE, BO.

Printing history: "Two Sermons Preached Before the Twenty-Eighth
Congregational Society in Boston," see A 33.

A 36.3.a
Third edition, first printing (1856)

Title page: SERMONS / OF / THEISM, ATHEISM, / AND / THE POPULAR
THEOLOGY. / BY / THEODORE PARKER, / MINISTER OF THE TWENTY-EIGHTH
CONGREGATIONAL SOCIETY IN BOSTON. / [rule] / SECOND EDITION. /
[rule] / BOSTON: / LITTLE, BROWN AND COMPANY. / 1856.

365pp. Deposit copy: BL (7 June 1858). Price, $1.25. *Locations:*
BL, MH, MH-AH, ScU.

A 36.3.b
Third edition, second printing (1859)

Two issues have been noted

A 36.3.b$_1$
First issue (1859)

Title page: The same as in the third edition, first printing,
except: 'SERMONS . . . BOSTON: / RUFUS LEIGHTON, JR. / 1859.'.

365pp. *Locations:* MH-AH, RPB.

A 36.3.b$_2$
Second issue (1861)

Title page: The same as in the third edition, first printing,
except: 'SERMONS . . . BOSTON. / THIRD EDITION. / BOSTON: / TICKNOR
AND FIELDS. / M DCCC LXI.'.

365pp. The title leaf is a cancel. *Location:* CtY.

A 36.3.c
Third edition, third printing (1864)

Title page: The same as in the third edition, second printing,
second issue, except: 'SERMONS . . . EDITION. / NEW YORK: /
PUBLISHED BY D. APPLETON & CO. / BOSTON: T. O. H. P. BURNHAM. /
1864.'.

365pp. *Location:* NIC (rebound).

A 36.3.d
Third edition, fourth printing (1870)

Title page: The same as in the third edition, first printing,
except: 'SERMONS . . . BOSTON. / FOURTH EDITION. / BOSTON: /
HORACE B. FULLER / 14, BROMFIELD STREET. / 1870.'.

365pp. Noted in *[Theodore Parker's Works]* binding (see B 2).
Inscribed copy: JM (25 December 1870). Price, $1.50. *Locations:*
JM, ViU.

A 36.4.a
Second English edition, first printing (1865)

Title page: SERMONS / OF / THEISM, ATHEISM, / AND / THE POPULAR
THEOLOGY. / BY / THEODORE PARKER. / LONDON: / TRÜBNER & CO., 60,
PATERNOSTER ROW. / 1865.

257pp. *Collected Works*, vol. 11 (see B 1). Deposit copy: BL
(6 October 1865). Price, 6s. *Locations:* BE, BL, BO, CtY, NcU.

A 36.4.b
Second English edition, second printing (1867)

Title page: The same as in the second English edition, first
printing, except: 'SERMONS . . . PARKER. / [gothic] Second
Edition. / LONDON: / N. TRÜBNER & CO., 60, PATERNOSTER ROW. /
1867'.

257pp. *Collected Works*, vol. 11 (see B 1). *Locations:* JM, MH-AH.

A 36.5
Fifth edition, only printing [1907]

Title page: THEISM, ATHEISM AND THE / POPULAR THEOLOGY / BY /
THEODORE PARKER / EDITED WITH A PREFACE / BY / CHARLES W. WENDTE /
[publisher's logo] / BOSTON / AMERICAN UNITARIAN ASSOCIATION / 25
BEACON STREET

389pp. *Centenary Edition*, vol. [2] (see B 3). MH-AH copy received
19 September 1910. *Locations:* InU, JM, MBAt, MH, MH-AH, NcU.

A 37   A SERMON OF OLD AGE
            1854

A 37.1

First edition, only printing (1854)

A SERMON OF OLD AGE, / PREACHED AT THE MUSIC HALL / ON SUNDAY, THE 29TH OF JANUARY, 1854. / [rule] / BY THEODORE PARKER, / Minister of the XXVIII. Congregational Society in Boston. / [rule] / PHONOGRAPHICALLY REPORTED BY RUFUS LEIGHTON. / BOSTON: / BENJAMIN B. MUSSEY & CO. / 1854.

Pagination: [1–5] 6–32.

Collation: [1]⁴ 2–4⁴.

Contents: p. 1: 'A SERMON OF OLD AGE.'; p. 2: blank; p. 3: title page; p. 4: printer's imprint; pp. 5–32: text.

Typography and paper: page size: 9 5/16" X 5 5/8"; text size: 6 3/8" X 5 11/16"; wove paper; 29 lines per page. No running heads.

Binding: light gray; light tan wrappers: recto: all within a double-rule frame: the same as the title page; front verso and back recto and verso: blank. All edges trimmed.

Printing: Prentiss and Sawyer, 19 Water Street, Boston.

Publication: Parker wrote a friend on 12 February 1854 that his sermon would "go to press to-morrow" (Weiss, *Life and Correspondence* [C 5], 2:124). Price, 15¢.

Locations: JM, MH, MH-AH.

A 37.2
Second edition, only printing (1859)

Title page: A SERMON OF OLD AGE, / PREACHED AT THE MUSIC HALL, / ON SUNDAY, JANUARY 29, 1854. / BY / THEODORE PARKER, / MINISTER OF THE TWENTY-EIGHTH CONGREGATIONAL SOCIETY IN BOSTON. / SECOND EDITION. / BOSTON: / PUBLISHED BY THE FRATERNITY. / 1859.

23pp. Wrappers. *Locations:* JM, MH, MH-AH.

A 38   THE NEBRASKA QUESTION
         1854

A 38

First edition, only printing (1854)

THE NEBRASKA QUESTION. / [rule] / SOME THOUGHTS / ON THE / [gothic]
New Assault upon Freedom in America, / AND THE / GENERAL STATE OF
THE COUNTRY / IN RELATION THEREUNTO, / SET FORTH IN A DISCOURSE
PREACHED AT THE MUSIC / HALL, IN BOSTON, ON MONDAY, FEB. 12,
1854. / BY THEODORE PARKER, / Minister of the XXVIII.
Congregational Society in Boston. / [rule] / BOSTON: / BENJAMIN B.
MUSSEY & CO. / 1854.

Pagination: [1–3] 4–72.

Collation: [1]^8 2–4^8 5^4.

Contents: p. 1: title page; p. 2: printer's imprint; pp. 3–72: text.

Typography and paper: page size: 9 3/8" X 5 13/16"; text size:
6 3/8" X 3 11/16"; wove paper; 33 lines per page. No running heads.

Binding: light gray; light tan wrappers: front recto: all within a
double-rule frame: the same as the title page; front verso and back
recto and verso: blank. All edges trimmed.

Printing: Prentiss and Sawyer, 19 Water Street, Boston.

Publication: Parker sent S. J. May a copy on [11] March 1854
(Octavius Brooks Frothingham, *Theodore Parker* [New York: Putnam's,
1874], p. 289). Inscribed copy: MBAt (from Parker, 15 September
1854).

Locations: JM, MBAt, MH, MH-AH, NcD.

Note one: "This Discourse is printed mainly from the phonographic report of Messrs. Yerrinton and Leighton.—March 7th, 1854" (p. 72).

Note two: The discourse was actually delivered on a Sunday.

96

A 39   AN ADDRESS DELIVERED BEFORE THE NEW YORK CITY
ANTI-SLAVERY SOCIETY
1854

A 39

First edition, only printing (1854)

AN ADDRESS / DELIVERED BY THE / REV. THEODORE PARKER, / BEFORE
THE / [gothic] New York City Anti-Slavery Society, / AT ITS / FIRST
ANNIVERSARY, / HELD AT THE / BROADWAY TABERNACLE, / May 12, 1854. /
NEW YORK: / AMERICAN ANTI-SLAVERY SOCIETY, / 142 NASSAU STREET. /
1854.

Pagination: [1–3] 4–46 [47–48].

Collation: [1]^6 2–4^6.

Contents: p. 1: title page; p. 2: blank; pp. 3–46: text; pp. 47–48:
blank.

Typography and paper: page size: 6" X 3 11/16"; text size: 4 7/16"
X 2 5/8"; wove paper; 33 lines per page. No running heads.

Binding: light purplish pink; very light tan wrappers: front recto:
all within a single wavy-rule frame with leaf-and-vine designs in
each corner: the same as the title page; front verso and back recto
and verso: blank. All edges trimmed.

Printing: Unknown.

Publication: MH copy received from Parker 7 June 1854.

Locations: BL, DLC, MH.

A 40   THE NEW CRIME AGAINST HUMANITY
           1854

A 40

First edition, only printing (1854)

THE NEW CRIME AGAINST HUMANITY. / [rule] / A / SERMON, / PREACHED
AT / THE MUSIC HALL, IN BOSTON, / ON SUNDAY, JUNE 4, 1854. /
[rule] / BY THEODORE PARKER, / Minister of the XXVIII.
Congregational Society. / [rule] / WITH THE LESSON OF THE DAY FOR
THE PREVIOUS SUNDAY. / BOSTON: / BENJAMIN B. MUSSEY & CO. / 1854.

Pagination: [1–3] 4–10 [11–13] 14–72 [73] 74–76.

Collation: [1]^4 2–9^4 10^2.

Contents: p. 1: title page; p. 2: printer's imprint and Parker's
note on the sermon, dated 10 June 1854; pp. 3–10: 'INTRODUCTORY.';
p. 11: 'THE NEW CRIME AGAINST HUMANITY.'; p. 12: blank; pp. 13–72:
text; pp. 73–76: 'APPENDIX.'.

Typography and paper: page size: 9 1/4" X 5 3/4"; text size:
"Introductory": 6 9/16" (6 1/4") X 3 3/4"; text: 6 5/8" (6 5/16")
X 3 11/16"; wove paper; "Introductory": 46 lines per page; text: 36
lines per page. Running heads: rectos: pp. 5–71: 'AGAINST
HUMANITY.'; p. 75: 'APPENDIX.'; versos: pp. 4–72: 'THE NEW CRIME';
pp. 74–76: 'APPENDIX.'.

Binding: light gray; light tan wrappers: front recto: all within a
double–rule frame: the same as the title page; front verso and back
recto and verso: blank. All edges trimmed.

Printing: Prentiss and Sawyer, 19 Water Street, Boston.

Publication: Price, 20¢.

Locations: DLC, JM, MBAt, MH, MH–AH.

A 41   THE LAW OF GOD AND THE STATUTES OF MEN
          1854

A 41

First edition, only printing (1854)

THE LAW OF GOD AND THE STATUTES OF MEN. / [ornate rule] / A / SERMON, / PREACHED AT / THE MUSIC HALL, IN BOSTON, / ON SUNDAY, JUNE 18, 1854. / [rule] / BY THEODORE PARKER, / Minister of the Twenty-Eighth Congregational Society. / [rule] / PHONOGRAPHICALLY REPORTED BY RUFUS LEIGHTON. / BOSTON: / BENJAMIN B. MUSSEY & CO. / 1854.

Pagination: [1–3] 4–32.

Collation: [1]^8 2^8.

Contents: p. 1: title page; p. 2: blank; pp. 3–32: text.

Typography and paper: page size: 9 1/8" X 5 3/4"; text size: 6 1/8" X 5 3/4"; wove paper; 28 lines per page. No running heads.

Binding: light tan wrappers: front recto: all within a triple-rule frame: the same as the title page, except: 'LAWS' is substituted for 'LAW' and 'Bazin & Chandler, Printers, 37 Cornhill, Boston.' is between the second and third frames at the bottom; front verso and back recto and verso: blank. All edges trimmed.

Printing: Bazin and Chandler, 37 Cornhill, Boston.

Publication: Price, 15¢.

Locations: DLC, JM, MH-AH.

A 42   A SERMON OF THE DANGERS WHICH THREATEN THE RIGHTS OF MAN
        IN AMERICA
        1854

A 42.1

First edition, only printing (1854)

A / SERMON / OF THE / DANGERS WHICH THREATEN THE RIGHTS OF MAN / IN
AMERICA; / PREACHED AT THE MUSIC HALL, / ON SUNDAY, JULY 2, 1854, /
BY THEODORE PARKER, / Minister of the XXVIII. Congregational
Society. / [PHONOGRAPHICALLY REPORTED BY MESSRS. YERRINTON AND
LEIGHTON.] / [rule] / BOSTON: / BENJAMIN B. MUSSEY & CO. / 1854.

Pagination: [1-3] 4-56.

Collation: [1]^4 2-7^4.

Contents: p. 1: title page; p. 2: printer's imprint; pp. 3-56: text.

Typography and paper: page size: 9 3/16" X 5 11/16"; text size:
6 3/16" X 3 11/16"; wove paper; 36 lines per page. No running
heads.

Binding: light gray; light tan wrappers: front recto: all within a
double-rule frame: the same as the title page; front verso and back
recto and verso: blank. All edges trimmed.

Printing: Prentiss and Sawyer, 19 Water Street, Boston.

Publication: Price, 20¢.

Locations: DLC, JM, MH-AH.

100

A 42.2

Second edition, only printing [1897]

Title page: [Old South Church logo at left for six lines] [gothic]
Old South Leaflets. / No. 80. / [rule] / The Dangers / from
Slavery. / By THEODORE PARKER. / [rule] / FROM A SERMON ON "THE
DANGERS WHICH THREATEN THE RIGHTS OF / MAN IN AMERICA," PREACHED
IN MUSIC HALL, BOSTON, / SUNDAY, JULY 2, 1854. / [rule] / [24 lines
of text]

20pp. (including excerpts from Ralph Waldo Emerson's 1860 address
on Parker [pp. 17–19]). Head title. Published by the Directors of
the Old South Work, Boston. *Old South Leaflets*, no. 80. Price,
5¢. *Locations:* InU, MHi, ViU.

A 43   A SERMON OF THE MORAL DANGERS INCIDENT TO PROSPERITY
1855

A 43

First edition, only printing (1855)

A / SERMON / OF THE / MORAL DANGERS INCIDENT TO PROSPERITY, /
PREACHED AT THE MUSIC HALL, IN BOSTON, / ON SUNDAY, NOVEMBER 5,
1854. / [rule] / BY THEODORE PARKER, / Minister of the Twenty–eighth
Congregational Society. / [rule] / [PHONOGRAPHICALLY REPORTED BY
RUFUS LEIGHTON.] / BOSTON: / BENJAMIN H. GREENE. / 1855.

Pagination: [1–3] 4–29 [30–32].

Collation: [1]^4 2–4^4.

Contents: p. 1: title page; p. 2: printer's imprint; pp. 3–29:
text; pp. 30–32: blank.

Typography and paper: page size: 9 5/16" X 5 3/4"; text size:
6 11/16" (6 5/16") X 3 11/16"; wove paper; 31 lines per page.
Running heads: rectos: pp. 5–29: 'INCIDENT TO PROSPERITY.'; versos:
pp. 4–28: 'THE MORAL DANGERS'.

Binding: light gray; light tan wrappers: front recto: all within a
double–rule frame: the same as the title page; front verso: blank;
back recto: all within a double–rule frame: advertisement for 10
works by Parker; back verso: blank. All edges trimmed.

Printing: Prentiss and Sawyer, 19 Water Street, Boston.

Publication: MH copy received 26 February 1855. Price, 15¢.

Locations: JM, MH, MH–AH.

A 44   A SERMON OF THE CONSEQUENCES OF AN IMMORAL PRINCIPLE AND
        FALSE IDEA OF LIFE
        1855

A 44

First edition, only printing (1855)

A / SERMON / OF THE / CONSEQUENCES OF AN IMMORAL PRINCIPLE / AND /
FALSE IDEA OF LIFE. / PREACHED AT THE MUSIC HALL, IN BOSTON, / ON
SUNDAY, NOVEMBER 26, 1854. / [rule] / BY THEODORE PARKER, / Minister
of the Twenty-eighth Congregational Society. / [rule] /
[PHONOGRAPHICALLY REPORTED BY RUFUS LEIGHTON.] / BOSTON: / BENJAMIN
H. GREENE. / 1855.

Pagination: [1-3] 4-32.

Collation: [1]^4 2-4^4.

Contents: p. 1: title page; p. 2: printer's imprint; pp. 3-32: text.

Typography and paper: page size: 9 1/2" X 5 7/8"; text size:
6 13/16" (6 5/16") X 3 11/16"; wove paper; 31 lines per page.
Running heads: rectos: pp. 5-31: 'AND FALSE IDEA OF LIFE.'; versos:
pp. 4-32: 'THE CONSEQUENCES OF AN IMMORAL PRINCIPLE'.

Binding: light gray; light tan wrappers: front recto: all within a
double-rule frame: the same as the title page; front verso and back
recto: blank; back verso: advertisement for 10 works by Parker.
All edges trimmed.

Printing: Prentiss and Sawyer, 19 Water Street, Boston.

Publication: MH copy received 26 February 1855.   Price, 15¢.

Locations: JM, MBAt, MCo, MH, MH-AH, MHi, RPB.

A 45   ADDITIONAL SPEECHES, ADDRESSES, AND OCCASIONAL SERMONS
1855

A 45.1.a

First edition, first printing (1855)

ADDITONAL SPEECHES, / ADDRESSES, / AND / OCCASIONAL SERMONS, / IN
TWO VOLUMES. / BY / THEODORE PARKER, / MINISTER OF THE TWENTY-EIGHTH
CONGREGATIONAL SOCIETY / IN BOSTON. / VOLUME I. [II.] / BOSTON: /
LITTLE, BROWN AND COMPANY. / 1855.

Pagination: vol. 1: [i–v] vi–ix [x–xi] xii [1–3] 4–15 [16–18]
19–105 [106–108] 109–129 [130–133] 134 [135] 136–137 [138] 139–293
[294–297] 298–380 [381–383] 384–435 [436]; vol. 2: [i–ii] [1–3]
4–70 [71–73] 74–83 [84–85] 86–178 [179–181] 182–212 [213–215]
216–293 [294–297] 298–337 [338–339] 340–370 [371–375] 376–411
[412–415] 416–443 [444–445] 446–448 [449–452].

Collation: vol. 1: [a]^6 1–36^6 37^2; vol. 2: [a]^1 1–37^6 38^4.

Contents: vol. 1: p. i: title page; p. ii: copyright information;
p. iii: dedication to Wendell Phillips; p. iv: blank; pp. v–ix:
'PREFACE.' dated 'April 3, 1855.'; p. x: blank; pp. xi–xii: contents
of vol. 1; p. 1: selection half-title; p. 2: blank; pp. 3–15:
"Speech at the Ministerial Conference"; p. 16: blank; p. 17:
selection half-title; p. 18: blank; pp. 19–105: "The Boston
Kidnapping"; p. 106: blank; p. 107: selection half-title; p. 108:
blank; pp. 109–129: "The Aspect of Freedom in America"; p. 130:
blank; p. 131: selection half-title; p. 132: blank; pp. 133–293:
"Discourse Occasioned by the Death of Daniel Webster" [p. 138:
blank]; p. 294: blank; p. 295: selection half-title; p. 296: blank;
pp. 297–380: "The Nebraska Question"; p. 381: selection half-title;
p. 382: blank; pp. 383–435: "Address Delivered . . . Before the New
York City Anti-Slavery Society"; p. 436: blank; vol. 2: p. i: title
page; p. ii: copyright information; pp. 1–2: contents of vol. 2;
p. 3: selection half-title; p. 4: blank; pp. 5–70: "Some Thoughts
on the Progress of America"; p. 71: selection half-title; p. 72:

blank; pp. 73–178: "The New Crime Against Humanity" [p. 84: blank];
p. 179: selection half-title; p. 180: blank; pp. 181–212: "The Law
of God and the Statutes of Men"; p. 213: selection half-title; p.
214: blank; pp. 215–293: "The Dangers Which Threaten the Rights of
Man in America"; p. 294: blank; p. 295: selection half-title; p.
296: blank; pp. 297–337: "Two Sermons Preached Before the Twenty-
Eighth Congregational Society. Sermon I"; p. 338: blank; pp. 339–
370: "Sermon II"; p. 371: selection half-title; p. 372: blank; pp.
373–411: "A Sermon of Woman" [p. 374: blank]; p. 412: blank; p. 413:
selection half-title; p. 414: blank; pp. 415–443: "A Sermon of Old
Age"; p. 444: blank; pp. 445–448: 'APPENDIX.'[to "The Boston
Kidnapping"]; p. 449: advertisement for works by Parker; pp. 450–
452: blank.

Typography and paper: page size: 7 11/16" X 4 3/4"; text size:
6 1/8" (5 13/16") X 3 1/4"; wove paper; "Preface": 31 lines per
page; text: 29 lines per page. Running heads: vol. 1: rectos: pp.
vii–ix: 'PREFACE.'; pp. 5–435: selection titles; versos: pp. vi–
viii: 'PREFACE.'; p. xii: 'CONTENTS.'; pp. 4–434: selection titles;
vol. 2: rectos: pp. 5–443: selection titles; p. 447: 'APPENDIX.';
versos: pp. 4–442: selection titles; pp. 446–448: 'APPENDIX.'.

Binding: Two styles have been noted:

> *Binding A:* dark gray blue AR cloth (coarse ribbed morocco);
> black; gray olive TR cloth (wavy-grain); front and back
> covers: blindstamped triple-rule frame with curved ornaments
> in each corner, with a 3 1/4" four-leaf design in the center;
> spine: blindstamped rules and floral design with goldstamped
> 'PARKER'S / ADDITIONAL / SPEECHES / VOL. I. [II.]'.
> Flyleaves in both volumes. Pale yellow endpapers. All edges
> trimmed.

> *Binding B:* black; dark grayish red C cloth (sand-grain);
> front and back covers: blindstamped triple-rule frame with
> lines connecting the corners of the second and third frames,
> outside of a single-rule frame with intersecting lines in

each corner; spine: blindstamped bands with goldstamped 'THEODORE PARKER'S / WORKS. / ADDITIONAL / SPEECHES / VOL. II. / [H. B. Fuller's logo]'. Flyleaves in both volumes. Brown coated endpapers. All edges trimmed. Undoubtedly a remainder binding; probably used for inclusion in *[Theodore Parker's Works]* (see B 2).

Printing: Allen and Farnham, Cambridge.

Publication: Deposited for copyright: title, 14 April 1855; book, 26 April 1855. MBAt copy received from Parker 30 November 1855. Listed in the *English Catalogue* as an importation at 16s. Price, $2.50 the set.

Locations: Binding A: MB, MBAt, NcU; Binding B: MH–AH, ViU (vol. 2).

Printing histories: "Speech at the Ministerial Conference in Boston, May 29, 1851," *Liberator*, 25 (18 May 1855): 80; "The Boston Kidnapping," see A 30; "The Aspect of Freedom in America. A Speech at the Massachusetts Anti–Slavery Celebration at Abington, July 5, 1852," *Liberator*, 22 (30 July 1852): 122; "A Discourse Occasioned by the Death of Daniel Webster," see A 31; "The Nebraska Question," see A 38; "An Address Delivered . . . Before the New York City Anti–Slavery Society," see A 39; "Some Thoughts on the Progress of America, and the Influence of Her Diverse Institutions. An Address Prepared for the Anti–Slavery Convention in Boston, May 31, 1854," unlocated; "The New Crime Against Humanity," see A 40; "The Law of God and the Statutes of Men," see A 41; "The Dangers Which Threaten the Rights of Man in America," see A 42; "Two Sermons Preached Before the Twenty–Eighth Congregational Society," see A 33; "A Sermon of the Public Function of Woman," see A 34; "A Sermon of Old Age," see A 37.

A 45.1.b
First edition, second printing (1859)

Two issues have been noted

106

A 45.1.b$_1$
First issue (1859)

Title page: The same as in the first printing, except: 'ADDITIONAL
. . . BOSTON: / RUFUS LEIGHTON, JR. / 1859.'.

435pp., 448pp. *Locations:* CSt (vol. 2), MB.

A 45.1.b$_2$
Second issue (1861)

Title page: ADDITIONAL / SPEECHES, ADDRESSES, / AND / OCCASIONAL
SERMONS, / BY / THEODORE PARKER, / MINISTER OF THE TWENTY-EIGHTH
CONGREGATIONAL SOCIETY, IN BOSTON. / IN TWO VOLUMES. / VOL. I.
[II.] / BOSTON: / TICKNOR AND FIELDS. / M DCCC LXI.

435pp., 448pp. The title leaf is a cancel. *Location:* MiU.

A 45.1.c
First edition, third printing (1864)

Title page: The same as in the first printing, except: 'ADDITIONAL
. . . SERMONS. / IN . . . [II.] / NEW YORK: / D. APPLETON AND
COMPANY. / BOSTON: T. O. H. P. BURNHAM. / 1864.'.

435pp., 448pp. Noted in *[Theodore Parker's Works]* binding (see
B 2). Inscribed copy: JM (September 1864) Price, $3.00 the set.
Location: JM.

A 45.1.d
First edition, fourth printing (1867)

Title page: The same as in the third printing, except: 'ADDITIONAL
. . . [II.] / BOSTON: / HORACE B. FULLER, / (SUCCESSOR TO WALKER,
FULLER, AND COMPANY,) / 245, WASHINGTON STREET. / 1867.

435pp., 448pp. Noted in *[Theodore Parker's Works]* binding (see
B 2). *Locations:* JM, ViU (vol. 1).

A 46   A DISCOURSE OF THE FUNCTION OF A TEACHER OF RELIGION IN THESE TIMES 1855

A 46.1.a
First edition, presumed first printing (1855)

A / DISCOURSE / OF THE / FUNCTION OF A TEACHER OF RELIGION / IN THESE TIMES, / PREACHED AT THE ORDINATION OF / MARSHALL G. KIMBALL, / *As Minister of the Free Church at Barre, Worcester County, Mass.* / ON WEDNESDAY, JUNE 13, 1855. / [rule] / BY THEODORE PARKER, / Minister of the Twenty-eighth Congregational Society in Boston. / [rule] / BOSTON: / BENJAMIN H. GREENE. / 1855.

Pagination: [1-3] 4-56.

Collation: [1]^4 2-7^4.

Contents: p. 1: title page; p. 2: blank; pp. 3-56: text.

Typography and paper: page size: 9 1/2" X 5 3/4"; text size: 6 5/8" (6 1/4") X 3 11/16"; wove paper; 31 lines per page. Running heads: rectos and versos: 'DISCOURSE.'.

Binding: Two styles have been noted, priority undetermined:

> *Binding A:* light tan wrappers: front recto: all within a double-rule frame: the same as the title page; front verso and back recto: blank; back verso: advertisement for 15 works by Parker, and an 'ERRATA.' note that 'Moses' should read 'Marshall' on p. 56.

> *Binding B:* The same as Binding A, except: back wrapper verso: blank.

Printing: Presumably Prentiss and Sawyer, 19 Water Street, Boston.

Publication: Price, 20¢.

Locations: Binding A: MH; Binding B: TxU.

Note one: The "Order of Exercises" is at the bottom of p. 56.

Note two: The minister being ordained was Moses (not "Marshall") G. Kimball.

A 46.1.b
First edition, presumed second printing (1855)

Title page: The same as in the presumed first printing.

56pp. Wrappers. The printer's imprint (Prentiss and Sawyer, 19 Water Street, Boston) is now on p. 2. *Location:* MH–AH.

A 46.1.c
First edition, third printing (1855)

Title page: The same as in the presumed first printing, except: 'A . . . OF / MOSES . . .'.

56pp. Wrappers (reading 'MOSES' for 'MARSHALL'). *Location:* MBAt (lacks back wrapper).

A 47 THE TRIAL OF THEODORE PARKER
1855

A 47.1.a
First edition, first printing (1855)

Two issues have been noted

A 47.1.a$_1$
First issue (1855)

THE TRIAL / OF / THEODORE PARKER, / FOR THE / "MISDEMEANOR" / OF /
[gothic] A Speech in Faneuil Hall against Kidnapping, / BEFORE THE
CIRCUIT COURT OF THE UNITED STATES, / AT BOSTON, APRIL 3, 1855. /
WITH / THE DEFENCE, / BY / THEODORE PARKER, / MINISTER OF THE
TWENTY-EIGHTH CONGREGATIONAL SOCIETY IN BOSTON. / BOSTON: /
PUBLISHED FOR THE AUTHOR. / 1855.

Pagination: [i–v] vi–viii [ix] x–xx [1] 2–221 [222–224].

Collation: [A]^6 B^4 [1]^6 2–18^6 19^4.

Contents: p. i: title page; p. ii: copyright information and
printer's imprint; p. iii: dedication to John Parker Hale and
Charles Mayo Ellis; p. iv: blank; pp. v–viii: 'PREFACE.' dated
BOSTON, *24th August*, 1855.'; pp. ix–xx: 'INTRODUCTION.'; pp. 1–221:
'DEFENCE.'; p. 222: six lines of errata; p. 223: advertisement for
17 works by Parker; p. 224: blank.

Typography and paper: page size: 9 1/2" X 6"; text size: "Preface"
and "Introduction": 7 1/2" (7 1/4") X 4 5/16"; text: 7 5/8"
(7 3/8") X 4 5/16"; wove paper; "Preface" and "Introduction": 34
lines per page; text: 44 lines per page. Running heads: rectos:
p. vii: 'PREFACE.'; pp. xi–xix: 'INTRODUCTION.'; pp. 3–221: topical
headings; versos: pp. vi–viii: 'PREFACE.'; pp. x–xx:
'INTRODUCTION.'; pp. 2–220: topical headings.

Binding: Three styles have been noted, priority of the first two undetermined:

> *Binding A:* brown T cloth (rib); dark gray green TZ cloth (ripple-grain); front and back covers: blindstamped quintuple-rule frame with a 4 1/4" oval ornament in the center; spine: blindstamped floral designs with goldstamped 'PARKER'S / DEFENCE.'. Flyleaves. Pale yellow; pale yellow coated endpapers. All edges trimmed.

> *Binding B:* the same as Binding A, except: medium brown TZ cloth (ripple-grain); front and back covers: blindstamped triple-rule frame with lines connecting the corners of the second and third frames, outside of a single-rule frame with intersecting lines in each corner.

> *Binding C:* dark purple C cloth (sand-grain); front and back covers: blindstamped double-rule frame; spine: goldstamped '[rule] / [gothic] The / TRIAL / OF / THEODORE / PARKER / [H. B. Fuller logo] / [rule]'. Flyleaves. Brown coated endpapers. All edges trimmed. Undoubtedly a remainder binding; this title was advertised in the *American Catalogue* for 1876 by Fuller at $1.50.

Printing: Allen and Farnham, Cambridge.

Publication: Parker first thought the book would come out in August (Weiss, *Life and Correspondence* [C 5], 2:149). Deposited for copyright: title, 2 November 1855; book, 26 November 1855. MBAt copy (rebound) received from Parker 30 November 1855.

Locations: Binding A: BL, JM, MH-AH; Binding B: MBAt; Binding C: ViU.

A 47.1.a$_2$
Second issue (1864)

Title page: The same as in the first printing, first issue, except: 'THE . . . BOSTON. / NEW YORK: / D. APPLETON AND COMPANY. / BOSTON: T. O. H. P. BURNHAM. / 1864.'.

222pp. The title leaf is a cancel. *Location:* NIC (rebound).

A 47.1.b
First edition, second printing [1970]

Title page: The same as in the first printing, first issue, except: 'THE . . . BOSTON. / [publisher's logo] / NEGRO UNIVERSITIES PRESS / NEW YORK'.

222pp. Facsimile reprinting. Deposit copy: DLC (2 September 1970). Price, $10.50. *Locations:* DLC, JM.

A 47.1.c
First edition, third printing (1971)

Title page: THE TRIAL OF THEODORE PARKER / WITH THE DEFENCE / By / THEODORE PARKER / *The Black Heritage Library Collection* / [publisher's logo to the left of the next two lines] BOOKS FOR LIBRARIES PRESS / FREEPORT, NEW YORK / 1971

222pp. Facsimile reprinting. Deposit copy: DLC (25 September 1971). Price, $10.00. *Locations:* DLC, ScU.

A 48   THE GREAT BATTLE BETWEEN SLAVERY AND FREEDOM
        1856

A 48

First edition, only printing (1856)

THE / GREAT BATTLE / BETWEEN / SLAVERY AND FREEDOM, / [gothic]
Considered in Two Speeches / DELIVERED BEFORE THE AMERICAN
ANTISLAVERY SOCIETY, AT NEW YORK, / MAY 7, 1856. / BY THEODORE
PARKER, / MINISTER OF THE TWENTY-EIGHTH CONGREGATIONAL SOCIETY IN
BOSTON. / [rule] / [gothic] Phonographically Reported. / [rule] /
BOSTON: / BENJAMIN H. GREENE, / 124, WASHINGTON STREET. / 1856.

Pagination: [1–5] 6–33 [34–37] 38–93 [94–96].

Collation: [1]^4 2–12^4.

Contents: p. 1: title page; p. 2: printer's imprint; p. 3: 'THE
PRESENT ASPECT / OF / THE ANTISLAVERY ENTERPRISE, / AND OF / THE
VARIOUS FORCES WHICH WORK THEREIN: / A SPEECH / DELIVERED ON THE
MORNING OF MAY 7.'; p. 4: William Lloyd Garrison's introduction to
Parker's speeches; pp. 5–33: text; p. 34: blank; p. 35: 'THE /
PRESENT CRISIS IN AMERICAN AFFAIRS: / THE SLAVEHOLDERS' ATTEMPT TO
WRENCH THE TERRITORIES FROM / THE WORKING PEOPLE, / AND / TO SPREAD
BONDAGE OVER ALL THE LAND: / A SPEECH / DELIVERED ON THE EVENING OF
MAY 7.'; p. 36: 11 lines of verse; pp. 37–93: text; pp. 94–96:
blank.

Typography and paper: page size: 9 5/8" X 5 3/4"; text size: 6 1/2"
X 3 5/8"; wove paper; 34 lines per page. No running heads.

Binding: light gray; light tan wrappers: front recto: all within a
triple-rule frame: the same as the title page; front verso: blank;
back recto: advertisement for 12 works by Parker; back verso:
advertisement for lithos from C. H. Brainard. All edges trimmed.

Printing: John Wilson and Son, 22 School Street, Boston.

Publication: Parker wrote Horace Mann on 27 June 1856 that this pamphlet was "in press" (Weiss, *Life and Correspondence* [C 5], 2:188).

Locations: CtY, MH, MH–AH.

114

A 49   A NEW LESSON FOR THE DAY
          1856

A 49
First edition, only printing (1856)

[gothic] A New Lesson for the Day: / A / SERMON / PREACHED AT THE
MUSIC HALL, IN BOSTON, / ON SUNDAY, MAY 25, 1856. / BY / THEODORE
PARKER, / MINISTER OF THE TWENTY-EIGHTH CONGREGATIONAL SOCIETY. /
[rule] / [gothic] Phonographically reported by Messrs. Yerrinton
and Leighton. / [rule] / BOSTON: / BENJAMIN H. GREENE, / 124,
WASHINGTON STREET. / 1856.

Pagination: [1-3] 4-40.

Collation: [1]^4 2-5^4.

Contents: p. 1: title page; p. 2: printer's imprint; pp. 3-40:
text.

Typography and paper: page size: 9 5/8" X 5 3/4"; text size: 6 1/2"
X 3 5/8"; wove paper; 35 lines per page. No running heads.

Binding: light gray; light tan wrappers; front recto: all within a
triple-rule frame: the same as the title page; front verso: blank;
back recto: advertisement for 12 works by Parker; back verso:
advertisement for prints by C. H. Brainard. All edges trimmed.

Printing: John Wilson and Son, 22 School Street, Boston.

Publication: Unknown.

Locations: DLC, JM, MH, MH-AH.

A 50   THE PRESENT ASPECT OF SLAVERY IN AMERICA
           1858

A 50
First edition, only printing (1858)

THE / PRESENT ASPECT OF SLAVERY IN AMERICA / AND / THE IMMEDIATE
DUTY OF THE NORTH: / A SPEECH / DELIVERED IN THE HALL OF THE STATE
HOUSE, / BEFORE THE MASSACHUSETTS ANTI-SLAVERY CONVENTION, / ON
FRIDAY NIGHT, JANUARY 29, 1858. / [rule] / BY THEODORE PARKER. /
[rule] / BOSTON: / BELA MARSH, / 14 BROMFIELD STREET. / 1858.

Pagination: [1-3] 4-44.

Collation: [1]^4 2-5^4 6^2.

Contents: p. 1: title page; p. 2: printer's imprint; pp. 3-44: text.

Typography and paper: page size: 9" X 5 11/16"; text size:
6 11/16" (6 5/16") X 3 11/16"; wove paper; 36 lines per page.
Running heads: rectos: pp. 5-43: 'OF SLAVERY IN AMERICA.'; versos:
pp. 4-42: 'THE PRESENT ASPECT OF'; p. 44: 'THE PRESENT ASPECT OF
SLAVERY IN AMERICA.'.

Binding: light gray, light tan wrappers: front recto: all within a
double-rule frame: the same as the title page; front verso and back
recto: blank; back verso: advertisement for 17 works by Parker.
All edges trimmed.

Printing: Prentiss, Sawyer, & Co., 19 Water Street, Boston.

Publication: Price, 20¢.

Locations: DLC, MBAt, MH.

A 51   A SERMON ON FALSE AND TRUE THEOLOGY
1858

A 51.1

First edition, only printing (1858)

A / SERMON / ON / FALSE AND TRUE THEOLOGY, / DELIVERED AT THE / MUSIC HALL, BOSTON, / ON / SUNDAY, FEBRUARY 14, 1858, / BY / REV. THEODORE PARKER. / [rule] / From the Boston Daily Bee Report. / [rule] / BOSTON: / PRINTED AT THE BOSTON DAILY BEE PRINTING HOUSE. / NO. 7 STATE STREET. / 1858.

Pagination: [1–3] 4–8.

Collation: [1]^4.

Contents: p. 1: title page; p. 2: blank; pp. 3–8: text.

Typography and paper: page size: 9 5/8" X 5 5/8"; text size: 8" X 4 5/8"; wove paper; double columns, 67 lines per column.   No running heads.

Binding: Cover title.   All edges trimmed.

Printing: Boston Daily Bee Printing House.

Publication: Price, 8¢.

Locations: MBAt, MH–AH, MHi, RPB.

A 51.2
Second edition, only printing (1858)

FALSE AND TRUE THEOLOGY. / [rule] / A / SERMON, / DELIVERED AT /
THE MUSIC HALL, BOSTON, / ON SUNDAY, FEBRUARY 14, 1858. / BY /
REV. THEODORE PARKER, / MINISTER OF THE TWENTY-EIGHTH CONGREGATIONAL
SOCIETY. / [rule] / REVISED BY THE AUTHOR. / [rule] / BOSTON: /
WILLIAM L. KENT AND COMPANY. / 1858.

Pagination: [1–3] 4–11 [12] 13–15 [16].

Collation: [1]^8.

Contents: p. 1: title page; p. 2: printer's imprint; pp. 3–11: text;
pp. 12–13: 'EXCESSES OF THE REVIVAL—THEODORE PARKER'S CASE" from
the 17 March 1858 *Boston Daily Bee*; p. 14: "This document was handed
to Mr. Parker in his pulpit on the morning of Sunday, March 7,
1858"; p. 15: document from the American Systematic Beneficence
Society"; p. 16: blank.

Typography and paper: page size: 9 1/16" X 5 3/4"; text size: 7 1/2"
X 4 3/8"; wove paper; double columns, 56 lines per column. No
running heads.

Binding: Cover title. All edges trimmed.

Printing: George C. Rand and Avery, 3 Cornhill, Boston; Cowles and
Company, Lithographers, 17 Washington Street, Boston.

Publication: Price, 8¢.

Locations: JM, MH, MH–AH.

Note: Parker wrote a friend on 24 April 1858 that his "revival
sermons" (A 51–A 53) had "sold 10,000 in ten days and the demand
still continues" (Weiss, *Life and Correspondence* [C 5], 2:224).

A 52   A FALSE AND TRUE REVIVAL OF RELIGION
        1858

A 52.1.a

First edition, first printing (1858)

A FALSE AND TRUE REVIVAL OF RELIGION. / [rule] / A / SERMON, /
DELIVERED AT MUSIC HALL, BOSTON, / ON SUNDAY, APRIL 4, 1858. / BY /
REV. THEODORE PARKER. / [rule] / PHONOGRAPHICALLY REPORTED BY JAMES
M. W. YERRINGTON *[sic]*. / [rule] / BOSTON: / PUBLISHED BY WILLIAM
L. KENT & CO. / 1858. / Geo. C. Rand & Avery, Printers, 3 Cornhill,
Boston.

Pagination: [1–3] 4–12.

Collation: [1]^6.

Contents: p. 1: title page; p. 2: copyright information and
publication note; pp. 3–12: text.

Typography and paper: page size: 9 1/4" X 5 3/4"; text size: 7 1/2"
X 4 3/8"; wove paper; double columns, 56 lines per column. No
running heads.

Binding: Cover title. All edges trimmed.

Printing: George C. Rand and Avery, 3 Cornhill, Boston.

Publication: Deposited for copyright: title, 6 April 1858; book,
7 May 1858. Price, 8¢.

Locations: BL, JM, MH-AH.

A 52.1.b
First edition, second printing (1858)

Title page: The same as in the first printing, except: 'A . . .
JAMES M. W. YERRINTON. / [rule] . . .'.

12pp. Cover title. *Locations:* MH, MH–AH.

A 53 THE REVIVAL OF RELIGION WHICH WE NEED
1858

A 53.1.a
First edition, presumed first printing (1858)

THE REVIVAL OF RELIGION WHICH WE NEED. / [rule] / A / SERMON, /
DELIVERED AT MUSIC HALL, BOSTON, / ON SUNDAY, APRIL 11, 1858. /
BY / REV. THEODORE PARKER, / MINISTER OF THE TWENTY-EIGHTH
CONGREGATIONAL SOCIETY. / [rule] / PHONOGRAPHICALLY REPORTED BY
JAMES M. W. YERRINTON. / [rule] / BOSTON: / PUBLISHED BY W. L.
KENT & COMPANY. / 1858.

Pagination: [1-3] 4-15 [16].

Collation: $[1]^8$.

Contents: p. 1: title page; p. 2: copyright information and
printer's imprint; pp. 3-15: text; p. 16: blank.

Typography and paper: page size: 9 1/8" X 5 7/8"; text size: 7 1/2"
X 4 3/8"; wove paper; double columns, 56 lines per column. No
running heads.

Binding: Cover title. All edges trimmed.

Printing: George C. Rand and Avery, 3 Cornhill, Boston; Cowles and
Company, Lithographers, 17 Washington Street, Boston.

Publication: Deposited for copyright: title, 12 April 1858; book,
7 May 1858. Price, 8¢.

Location: JM.

A 53.1.b
First edition, presumed second printing (1858)

Title page: The same as in the presumed first printing, except: 'THE . . . 1858. / [rule] / Geo. C. Rand & Avery, Printers, 3 Cornhill, Boston.'.

15pp. Cover title. The printer's imprint is not present on p. 2. *Locations:* BL, JM, MBAt, MH, MH-AH.

A 53.1.c

First edition, third printing (1859)

Title page: The same as in the presumed first printing, except: 'THE . . . BOSTON: / PUBLISHED BY BELA MARSH, / 14 BROMFIELD STREET. / 1859.'.

15pp. Cover title. *Location:* RPB.

122

A 54   THE RELATION OF SLAVERY TO A REPUBLICAN FORM OF
        GOVERNMENT
        1858

A 54

First edition, only printing (1858)

THE RELATION OF SLAVERY TO A REPUBLICAN FORM OF GOVERNMENT. /
[rule] / A / SPEECH / DELIVERED AT THE / [gothic] New England
Anti-Slavery Convention, / WEDNESDAY MORNING, MAY 26, 1858. /
BY THEODORE PARKER. / [rule] / REVISED BY THE AUTHOR. / [rule] /
BOSTON: / WILLIAM L. KENT & COMPANY, 3 STATE STREET. / 1858.

Pagination: [1-3] 4-21 [22-24].

Collation: [1]^{12}.

Contents: p. 1: title page; p. 2: copyright information and
printer's imprint; pp. 3-21: text; pp. 22-24: blank.

Typography and paper: page size: 9 1/16" X 5 3/4"; text size: 7 1/2"
X 4 3/8"; wove paper; double columns, 56 lines per column. No
running heads.

Binding: Cover title. All edges trimmed.

Printing: George C. Rand and Avery, 3 Cornhill, Boston.

Publication: Price, 8¢.

Locations: BL, MBAt, TxU.

A 55   THE BIBLICAL, THE ECCLESIASTICAL, AND THE PHILOSOPHICAL
         NOTION OF GOD, AND THE SOUL'S NORMAL DELIGHT IN HIM
         1858

A 55

First edition, only printing (1858)

[two lines in gothic] The Biblical, the Ecclesiastical, and the
Philosophical Notion of God, / and the Soul's Normal Delight in
Him. / [rule] / FOUR SERMONS, / PREACHED IN THE / [gothic] Yearly
Meeting of Progressive Friends, / AT / LONGWOOD, PA., MAY 30TH AND
31ST, 1858. / BY / THEODORE PARKER, / *Minister of the XXVIIIth.*
Congregational Society in Boston. / [ornamental rule] / NEW YORK: /
JOHN F. TROW, PRINTER, 377 & 379 BROADWAY, / CORNER OF WHITE
STREET. / 1858.

Pagination: [1–3] 4–51 [52].

Collation: [1]^8 2–3^8 4^2.

Contents: p. 1: title page; p. 2: introductory remarks; pp. 3–14:
Sermon 1: "The Progressive Development of the Conception of God in
the Books of the Bible"; pp. 15–27: Sermon 2: "The Ecclesiastical
Conception of God, and Its Relation to the Scientific and Religious
Wants of Man"; pp. 28–40: Sermon 3: "The Philosophical Idea of God
and Its Relation to the Scientific and Religious Wants of Mankind
Now"; pp. 41–51: Sermon 4: "Of the Soul's Normal Delight in the
Infinite God"; p. 52: blank.

Typography and paper: page size: 9" X 5 5/8"; text size: 6 1/2" X
3 3/4"; wove paper; 47 lines per page. No running heads.

Binding: light gray; light tan wrappers: front recto: all within a
double-rule frame: the same as the title page, except: '[gothic]
The . . . [ornamental rule] / BOSTON: / BELA MARSH, / 14 BROMFIELD
STREET. / 1858.'; front verso and back recto: blank; back verso:
advertisement for 17 works by Parker. All edges trimmed.

Printing: John F. Trow, 377 and 379 Broadway, New York.

Publication: Price, 17 1/2¢.

Locations: JM, MH, MH-AH.

Note one: All four sermons were reprinted in 'PROCEEDINGS / OF THE / [gothic] Pennsylvania Yearly Meeting / OF / PROGRESSIVE FRIENDS, / INCLUDING / FOUR SERMONS BY THEODORE PARKER. / [wavy rule] / 1858. / [wavy rule] / [two lines of verse] / NEW YORK: / JOHN F. TROW, / PRINTER, 377 & 379 BROADWAY, / CORNER OF WHITE STREET. / 1858.', pp. 49-62, 62-75, 75-88, 89-100. Wrappers. *Locations:* CtY, MBAt.

Note two: All four sermons were also reprinted in '[gothic] Conference of Progressive Thinkers. / [rule] / [rule] / BREAD CAST UPON THE WATERS / BY / SOWERS OF THOUGHT, FOR THE CHURCH / OF THE FUTURE. / [rule] / WITH FOUR SERMONS BY THEODORE PARKER. / [rule] / [gothic] London: / GEORGE MANWARING, / *(Successor to JOHN CHAPMAN),* / 8, KING WILLIAM STREET, STRAND. / [rule] / 1860.', pp. 42-50, 51-59, 59-68, 68-75. Wrappers. *Location:* DLC.

A 56   THE EFFECT OF SLAVERY ON THE AMERICAN PEOPLE
         1858

A 56

First edition, only printing (1858)

THE EFFECT OF SLAVERY ON THE AMERICAN PEOPLE. / [rule] / A /
SERMON / PREACHED AT / THE MUSIC HALL, BOSTON, / ON SUNDAY, JULY 4,
1858, / BY / REV. THEODORE PARKER, / MINISTER OF THE TWENTY-EIGHTH
CONGREGATIONAL SOCIETY. / [rule] / REVISED BY THE AUTHOR. / [rule] /
BOSTON: / WILLIAM L. KENT & COMPANY, 3 STATE STREET. / 1858.

Pagination: [1-3] 4-14 [15-16].

Collation: [1]⁸.

Contents: p. 1: title page; p. 2: copyright information and
printer's imprint; pp. 3-14: text; p. 15: advertisement for three
works by Parker; p. 16: advertisement for 29 works by Parker.

Typography and paper: page size: 9 1/8" X 5 3/4"; text size: 7 1/2"
X 4 3/8"; wove paper; double columns, 56 lines per column.   No
running heads.

Binding: Cover title. All edges trimmed.

Printing: George C. Rand and Avery, 3 Cornhill, Boston.

Publication: Deposited for copyright: title, 13 July 1858.   Price,
8¢.

Locations: DLC, JM, MBAt, MH, MH-AH.

126

A 57   A SERMON FOR MIDSUMMER DAY
          1859

A 57

First edition, only printing (1859)

A SERMON FOR MIDSUMMER DAY. / [rule] / BEAUTY IN THE WORLD OF
MATTER, / CONSIDERED AS / A REVELATION OF GOD. / BY / THEODORE
PARKER, / MINISTER OF THE TWENTY-EIGHTH CONGREGATIONAL SOCIETY. /
PREACHED AT THE MUSIC HALL, / ON SUNDAY, JULY 15, 1855. / BOSTON: /
PUBLISHED BY THE FRATERNITY. / 1859.

Pagination: [1-3] 4-6 [7] 8-24.

Collation: [1]^6 2^6.

Contents: p. 1: title page; p. 2: printer's imprint; pp. 3-6:
'PREFATORY LETTER.' dated 'FRIEDRIKSSTAD, Santa Cruz, March 15,
1859.'; pp. 7-24: text.

Typography and paper: page size: 7 5/8" X 4 7/8"; text size:
"Prefatory Letter": 5 7/16" X 3 1/2"; text: 5 3/4" X 3 1/2"; wove
paper; "Prefatory Letter": 34 lines per page; text: 36 lines per
page. No running heads.

Binding: light purple; light purple coated; light tan wrappers:
front recto: all within a double-rule frame: the same basic
wording as the title page, but reset and with the following changes:
'A . . . GOD, / BY . . . 1855. / WITH PREFATORY LETTER FROM MR.
PARKER AT SANTA CRUIZ. / [rule] . . . FRATERNITY. / Sold by H. W.
Swett & Co., 128 Washington Street. / 1859.'; front verso:
advertisement for three books by Parker; back recto: advertisement
for five books by Parker; back verso: advertisement for 25 pamphlets
by Parker. All edges trimmed.

Printing: Allen and Farnham, Cambridge.

Publication: Price, 6¢.

Locations: BL, CtY, JM, MH, MH-AH.

128

A 58   THEODORE PARKER'S EXPERIENCE AS A MINISTER
        1859

A 58.1.a

First edition, first printing (1859)

THEODORE PARKER'S / EXPERIENCE AS A MINISTER, / WITH / SOME ACCOUNT
OF HIS EARLY LIFE, / AND / EDUCATION FOR THE MINISTRY; / CONTAINED
IN A LETTER FROM HIM TO THE MEMBERS OF THE / TWENTY-EIGHTH
CONGREGATIONAL SOCIETY OF BOSTON. / [rule] / BOSTON: / RUFUS
LEIGHTON, JR. / 1859.

Pagination: [i–iii] iv–v [vi] [7] 8–9 [10–11] 12–18 [19] 20–21
[22–25] 26–182 [183–188].

Collation: [1]^6 2^6 [3]^6 4–15^6 16^4.

Contents: p. i: title page; p. ii: copyright information and
printer's imprint; pp. iii–v: 'PREFACE.'; p. vi: blank; pp. 7–9:
'FAREWELL LETTER.' dated 'EXETER PLACE, 27th January, 1859.'; p. 10:
blank; pp. 11–18: 'LETTER TO MR. PARKER.'; pp. 19–21: 'REPLY OF MR.
PARKER / [rule] / FREDERICKSTED, SANTA CRUZ, 9th May, 1859.'; p. 22:
Parker's cover letter to the following text; p. 23: 'THEODORE
PARKER'S / EXPERIENCE AS A MINISTER.'; p. 24: blank; pp. 25–182:
'LETTER.' dated 'April 19th, 1859.'; p. 183: advertisement for three
works by Parker; p. 184: advertisement for five works by Parker; p.
185: advertisement for 26 works by Parker; pp. 186–188: blank.

Typography and paper: page size: 7 7/8" X 4 7/8"; text size: 5 7/8"
(5 1/2") X 3 5/16"; wove paper; 28 lines per page. Running heads:
rectos and versos: section titles.

Binding: Four styles have been noted, priority undetermined:

> *Binding A:* light brown TZ cloth (ripple-grain); front and
> back covers: blindstamped single-rule frame, outside of a
> double-rule frame with intersecting corners and sides, with

a 2 1/2" triangular design in the center; spine: blindstamped designs with goldstamped lettering: '[band] / [rule] / [rule] / THEODORE / PARKER'S / EXPERIENCE / AS A / MINISTER / [rule] / [rule] / [band]'. Flyleaves. Brown coated endpapers. All edges trimmed.

Binding B: the same as Binding A, except: medium brown BD cloth (bead-grain); light brown TZ cloth (ripple-grain); front and back covers: blindstamped triple-rule frame with lines connecting the corners of the second and third frames, outside of a single-rule frame with intersecting lines in each corner, with a 2 1/4" triangular design in the center.

Binding C: medium brown BD cloth (bead-grain); front and back covers: blindstamped triple-rule frame with lines connecting the corners of the second and third frames, outside of a single-rule frame with intersecting lines in each corner, with a goldstamped 3 1/4" leaf-and-vine design in the center; spine: goldstamped '[band] / [rule] / [rule] / THEODORE / PARKER'S / EXPERIENCE / AS A / MINISTER / [heraldic-like design] / [heraldic-like design] / [heraldic-like design] / [rule] / [rule] / [band]'. Flyleaves. Brown coated endpapers. All edges trimmed.

Binding D: light red-pink wrappers: front recto: all within a double-rule frame: the same as the title page; front verso and back recto and verso: blank. Wrappers are pasted over stiff white endpapers. All edges trimmed.

Printing: Electrotyped by Cowles and Company, 17 Washington Street, Boston; printed by George C. Rand and Avery, 3 Cornhill, Boston.

Publication: Deposited for copyright: title and book, 2 July 1859. Inscribed copies: MB (Binding B, from Rufus Leighton, 8 July 1859); JM (Binding C, 25 July 1859); JM (Binding B, 17 August 1859); MB (Binding B, presentation slip from Parker, 24 August 1859); ViU (rebound; August 1859).

Locations: Binding A: JM, MH; Binding B: JM, MB; Binding C: JM, MB, MH; Binding D: JM, MH–AH.

A 58.1.b
First edition, second printing (1860)

Title page: The same as in the first printing, except: 'THEODORE . . . JR. / 1860.'.

182pp. *Locations:* JM, MH–AH.

A 58.2

Presumed first English edition, only printing (1859)

THEODORE PARKER'S / EXPERIENCE AS A MINISTER, / WITH / [gothic]
Some Account of his Early Life / AND / EDUCATION FOR THE MINISTRY, /
CONTAINED IN / A LETTER FROM HIM TO THE MEMBERS OF THE TWENTY- /
EIGHTH CONGREGATIONAL SOCIETY OF BOSTON. / [rule] / LONDON: / E. T.
WHITFIELD, 178, STRAND. / 1859.

Pagination: [i–iii] iv–xvi [1] 2–128.

Collation: [A]^8 B–I^8.

Contents: p. i: title page; p. ii: printer's imprint; pp. iii–xvi:
the same as pp. iii–22 of the first edition; pp. 1–128: text.

Typography and paper: page size: 6 11/16" X 4 1/8"; text size:
5 7/16" (5 3/16") X 3"; wove paper; 34 lines per page. Running
heads: rectos and versos: section titles.

Binding: Gray violet BD cloth (bead–grain); front and back covers:
blindstamped triple–rule frame with ornaments in each corner; spine:
blindstamped rules at top and bottom with goldstamped 'PARKER'S /
EXPERIENCE / AS A / MINISTER / WHITFIELD'. Pale yellow endpapers.
All edges trimmed.

Printing: John Edward Taylor, Little Queen Street, Lincoln's Inn
Fields, London.

Publication: Deposit copy: BL (18 November 1859). Price, 2s6d.

Location: BL.

Note: A 16–page catalogue of Whitfield's publications, dated
November 1859, is inserted at the back.

A 58.3.a

Presumed second English edition, first printing (1859)

THEODORE PARKER'S / EXPERIENCE AS A MINISTER. / WITH / SOME ACCOUNT OF HIS EARLY LIFE, / AND / EDUCATION FOR THE MINISTRY. / LONDON: / [rule] / 1859.

Pagination: [i–iii] iv [v–vi] 7–8 [9] 10 [11] 12–79 [80].

Collation: [A]^8 B–E^8.

Contents: p. i: title page; p. ii: printer's imprint; pp. iii–10: the same as pp. iii–22 of the first edition; pp. 11–79: text; p. 80: ornament.

Typography and paper: page size: 7 5/16" X 4 13/16"; text size: 5 15/16" (5 11/16") X 3 7/16"; wove paper; 49 lines per page. Running heads: rectos and versos: section titles.

Binding: light tan wrappers: front recto: all except the first line within a double-rule frame with floral ornaments in each corner and at the sides: 'PEOPLE'S EDITION—UNABRIDGED. / THEODORE PARKER'S / EXPERIENCE AS A MINISTER. / WITH / SOME ACCOUNT OF HIS EARLY LIFE, / AND / EDUCATION FOR THE MINISTRY. / [rule] / [rule] / [12-line blurb by W. Forster] / PRICE ONE SHILLING. / LONDON: / JOHN CHAPMAN, / No. 8, KING WILLIAM STREET, STRAND. / MDCCCLIX.'; front verso and back recto and verso: blank. All edges trimmed.

Printing: John Watts, Fleet Street, E.C., London.

Publication: Published by John Chapman, London. Deposit copy: BL (26 November 1859). *People's Edition.* Price, 1s.

Location: BL.

A 58.3.b

Presumed second English edition, second printing (1860)

Title page: The same as in the presumed second English edition,
first printing, except: 'THEODORE . . . MINISTRY. / (THIRD
THOUSAND.) / LONDON: / JOHN CHAPMAN, / No. 8, KING WILLIAM STREET,
STRAND. / MDCCCLX.'.

79pp. Presumed wrappers. *Location:* MH (rebound).

Note: No copies of the second thousand have been located.

134

A 59   A SERMON FOR THE NEW YEAR
         1859

A 59

First edition, only printing (1859)

A SERMON FOR THE NEW YEAR. / [rule] / WHAT RELIGION / MAY DO FOR A
MAN. / BY / REV. THEODORE PARKER, / MINISTER OF THE TWENTY-EIGHTH
CONGREGATIONAL SOCIETY. / PREACHED AT THE MUSIC HALL, / ON SUNDAY,
JAN. 2, 1859. / [rule] / PHONOGRAPHICALLY REPORTED BY RUFUS
LEIGHTON. / [rule] / BOSTON: / PUBLISHED BY THE FRATERNITY. / 1859.

Pagination: [1-3] 4-23 [24].

Collation: [1]^6 2^6.

Contents: p. 1: title page; p. 2: printer's imprint; pp. 3-22: text;
pp. 22-23: "Farewell Letter"; p. 24: blank.

Typography and paper: page size: 7 3/4" X 4 7/8"; text size: 5 5/8"
X 3 7/16"; wove paper; 35 lines per page. No running heads.

Binding: Two styles have been noted, priority undetermined:

    Binding A: Cover title. All edges trimmed.

    Binding B: light green; pale pink wrappers: front recto: all
    within a double-rule frame: the same as the title page,
    except: 'A . . . BY / [next two lines reset in a larger
    size type than on the title page] REV. THEODORE PARKER, /
    MINISTER OF THE TWENTY-EIGHTH CONGREGATIONAL SOCIETY. /
    PREACHED . . . 1859. / PHONOGRAPHICALLY REPORTED BY RUFUS
    LEIGHTON. / [rule] . . . FRATERNITY. / Sold by H. W. Swett,
    128 Washington Street. / 1859.'; front verso: advertisement
    for three books by Parker; back recto: advertisement for
    five books by Parker; back verso: advertisement for 25
    pamphlets by Parker. All edges trimmed.

Printing: Allen and Farnham, Cambridge.

Publication: Price, 6¢.

Locations: Binding A: JM, MBAt; Binding B: JM, MH, MH-AH.

A 60   THE TWO CHRISTMAS CELEBRATIONS
         1859

A 60

First edition, only printing (1859)

THE / TWO CHRISTMAS CELEBRATIONS, / A.D. I AND MDCCCLV. / A /
CHRISTMAS STORY / FOR / MDCCCLVI. / BY THEODORE PARKER, / *Minister
of the* 28*th Congregational Society of Boston.* / BOSTON: / RUFUS
LEIGHTON, JR. / 1859.

Pagination: [1–3] 4–46 [47–48].

Collation: [1]^4 2–6^4.

Contents: p. 1: title page; p. 2: copyright information and
printer's imprint; pp. 3–46: text; pp. 47–48: blank.

Typography and paper: page size: 7 7/16" X 5 1/2"; text size: 5 1/2"
(5 3/16") X 3 7/16"; wove paper; 23 lines per page. Running heads:
rectos and versos: 'TWO CHRISTMAS CELEBRATIONS.'.

Binding: medium brown A cloth (ribbed morocco); gray green coarse
BD cloth (bead-grain); very purplish blue; medium brown; deep red
TZ cloth (ripple-grain); front cover: blindstamped triple-rule
frame with an intersecting-lines design inside each corner, with a
goldstamped 3 1/2" wreath around 'TWO / CHRISTMAS / CELEBRATIONS' in
the center; back cover: the same as the front cover, except all
blindstamped; spine: blank. Flyleaves. Light brown; brown coated
endpapers. All edges trimmed.

Printing: H. O. Houghton and Company, Cambridge.

Publication: Deposited for copyright: title and book: 16 December
1859. Deposit copy: DLC (16 December 1859). Inscribed copy: MB
(rebound; from Rufus Leighton, 25 December 1859).

Locations: CSt, DLC, JM, MB, MBAt, MH, ViU.

A 61   JOHN BROWN'S EXPEDITION REVIEWED
         1860

A 61

First edition, only printing (1860)

JOHN BROWN'S EXPEDITION / REVIEWED IN / A LETTER FROM / REV.
THEODORE PARKER, / AT ROME, / TO / FRANCIS JACKSON, / BOSTON. /
[rule] / BOSTON: / PUBLISHED BY THE FRATERNITY. / 1860.

Pagination: [1–3] 4–19 [20].

Collation: [1^6 2^4].

Contents: p. 1: title page; p. 2: printer's imprint; pp. 3–19: text;
p. 20: blank.

Typography and paper: page size: 7 5/8" X 4 5/8"; text size:
5 7/16" X 3 5/16"; wove paper; 34 lines per page. No running heads.

Binding: light gray; light tan wrappers: front recto: all within a
double-rule frame: the same as the title page; front verso and back
recto and verso: blank. All edges trimmed.

Printing: George C. Rand and Avery, 3 Cornhill, Boston.

Publication: Unknown.

Locations: DLC, JM, MH, MH-AH, NcD.

138

A 62   THE MATERIAL CONDITION OF THE PEOPLE OF MASSACHUSETTS
          1860

A 62
First edition, only printing (1860)

THE / MATERIAL CONDITION / OF THE / PEOPLE OF MASSACHUSETTS / BY /
REV. THEODORE PARKER. / REPRINTED FROM THE CHRISTIAN EXAMINER. /
BOSTON: / PUBLISHED BY THE FRATERNITY. / 1860.

Pagination: [1–3] 4–52.

Collation: [1]^6 2–4^6 5^2.

Contents: p. 1: title page; p. 2: note on reprinting and printer's
information; pp. 3–52: text.

Typography and paper: page size: 7 9/16" X 4 13/16"; text size:
5 1/8" X 3 3/8"; wove paper; 35 lines per page. No running heads.

Binding: light brown wrappers; front recto: all within a double–rule
frame: the same as the title page, except: 'THE . . .
MASSACHUSETTS. / BY . . . FRATERNITY. / FOR SALE BY BELA MARSH, 114
BROMFIELD STREET. / 1860.'; front verso and back recto and verso:
blank. All edges trimmed.

Printing: George C. Rand and Avery, 3 Cornhill, Boston.

Publication: Unknown.

Location: JM.

Note: Reprinted from the *Christian Examiner*, 65 (July 1858): 19–60.

A 63   PRAYERS
1862

A 63.1.a
First edition, presumed first printing (1862)

PRAYERS / BY / THEODORE PARKER / BOSTON / WALKER, WISE AND COMPANY /
1862

Pagination: [i–iv] [i–iii] iv [5] 6–200.

Collation: [a]^2 [1]^8 2–12^8 13^4.

Contents: pp. i–ii: blank; inserted leaf with engraving of Parker
printed on verso; p. iii: title page; p. iv: copyright information
and printer's imprint; p. i: dedication to Lydia Parker; p. ii:
blank; pp. iii–iv: 'PREFACE.' signed 'R. L. / M. G. / *Boston,
September* 26, 1861.'; pp. 5–200: text.

Typography and paper: page size: 6 15/16" X 4 1/2"; text size:
4 1/2" X 3"; laid paper with vertical chain lines 1 1/2" apart; 29
lines per page. No running heads.

Binding: medium brown AR cloth (coarse ribbed morocco); front and
back covers: blindstamped triple-rule frame; spine: blindstamped
'[rule] / [band] / [rule]' at the top and bottom, with goldstamped
'PRAYERS / [rule] / PARKER'. Front or back flyleaf. Brown coated
endpapers. All edges trimmed. Top edges gilded.

Printing: Stereotyped and printed by H. O. Houghton, Cambridge.

Publication: Inscribed copies: JM (14 June 1862); MB (rebound; from
Rufus Leighton, June 1862). Listed in the *English Catalogue* as an
importation at 5s6d. Price, 75¢.

Locations: JM, MH–AH.

Note: Edited by Rufus Leighton and Matilda Goddard.

A 63.1.b

First edition, presumed second printing (1862)

Title page: The same as in the presumed first printing.

200pp. The same as in the first printing, except:

Pagination: [i–iv] [i–iii] iv [5] 6–200 [201–202].

Collation: [a]^2 [1]^8 2–12^8 13^6 $_{(-13_6)}$.

Contents: pp. i–iv, i–200: the same as in the presumed first printing; pp. 201–202: blank.

Publication: Inscribed copy: JM (15 November 1862).

Locations: JM, MH.

Note: Leaf 13$_6$ is cancelled and the stub is pasted under the rear pastedown endpaper.

A 63.1.c

First edition, third printing (1863)

Title page: The same as in the presumed first printing, except: 'PRAYERS . . . COMPANY / 1863'.

200pp. *Locations:* JM, MH.

A 63.1.d

First edition, fourth printing (1870)

Title page: The same as in the presumed first printing, except: 'PRAYERS . . . PARKER / BOSTON: / WILLIAM V. SPENCER. / 1870.'.

200pp. Price, $2.00. *Locations:* MBAt, MH.

A 63.1.e

First edition, fifth printing (1874)

Title page: The same as in the fourth printing, except: 'PRAYERS
. . . BOSTON: / JAMES CAMPBELL. / 1874.'.

200pp. *Location:* MB.

A 63.1.f

First edition, sixth printing (1882)

Title page: PRAYERS / BY / THEODORE PARKER / [gothic] A New
Edition / WITH A PREFACE BY LOUISA M. ALCOTT, AND / A MEMOIR BY
F. B. SANBORN / [rule] / BOSTON / ROBERTS BROTHERS / 1882

200pp. 500 copies printed on 10 January 1882; 500 copies printed
on 16 May 1882. Deposit copy: BL (17 July 1882). Inscribed copy:
MH (from F. B. Sanborn, 25 January 1882). MH-AH copy (rebound)
received 30 January 1882. Listed in the *English Catalogue* as an
importation at 5s. Price, $1.00. *Locations:* BL, CtY, MH.

A 63.1.g

First edition, seventh printing (1886)

Title page: The same as in the sixth printing, except: 'PRAYERS
. . . BROTHERS / 1888'.

200pp. 280 copies printed on 21 February 1888. *Location:* JM.

A 63.1.h

First edition, eighth printing (1892)

Title page: The same as in the sixth printing, except: 'PRAYERS
. . . BROTHERS / 1892'.

200pp. 280 copies printed on 26 March 1892. *Locations:* JM, MH.

A 63.1.i

First edition, ninth printing (1901)

Title page: The same as in the sixth printing, except: 'PRAYERS
. . . BOSTON / AMERICAN UNITARIAN ASSOCIATION / 1901'.

200pp. Price, 75¢. Inscribed copy: MH–AH (28 November 1902).
Location: MH–AH.

A 63.1.j

First edition, tenth printing (1906)

Title page: The same as in the ninth printing, except: 'PRAYERS
. . . ASSOCIATION / 1906'.

200pp. *Location:* JM.

A 63.2

First English edition, only printing (1862)

PRAYERS / BY / THEODORE PARKER. / WHITFIELD: STRAND, LONDON. /
MATTHEWS: BENNETT'S HILL, BIRMINGHAM. / [rule] / 1862.

Pagination: [i–iv] [i–iii] iv [5] 6–184.

Collation: [a]² [A]⁸ B–K⁸ L⁴.

Contents: pp. i–ii: blank; p. iii: title page; p. iv: blank; p. i:
dedication; p. ii: blank; pp. iii–iv: 'PREFACE.'; pp. 5–184: text.

Typography and paper: page size: 6 15/16" X 4 11/16"; text size:
5 1/16" X 2 15/16"; wove paper; 29 lines per page. No running
heads.

Binding: medium brown AR-like cloth (coarse ribbed morocco); front
and back covers: blindstamped double-rule frame; spine: goldstamped
'PRAYERS / [rule] / [rule] / PARKER'. Yellow endpapers. All edges
trimmed.

Printing: M. Billing, Livery Street, Birmingham, England.

Publication: Deposit copy: BL (19 November 1862). Price, 2s.

Locations: BC, BE, BL, BO.

A 63.3.a

Second English edition, first printing (1863)

Combined with *Ten Sermons of Religion* (London: Trübner, 1863) in
two-volumes-in-one format; see A 32.3.a for further information.

A 63.3.b

Second English edition, second printing (1879)

Combined with *Ten Sermons of Religion* (London: Trübner, 1879) in two-volumes-in-one format; see A 32.3.b for further information.

A 63.4

Fourth edition, only printing (1910)

Title page: PRAYERS. / BY / THEODORE PARKER / [gothic] London / THE BRITISH & FOREIGN UNITARIAN ASSOCIATION / ESSEX HALL, ESSEX STREET, STRAND, W.C. / 1910

116pp. Edited by Charles Hargrove. Published June 1910. Deposit copies: BL (27 May 1910); BO (11 June 1910). Price, 1s. *Locations:* BL, BO.

A 64   LESSONS FROM THE WORLD OF MATTER AND THE WORLD OF MAN
         1865

A 64.1.a

First edition, first printing (1865)

[red] LESSONS / FROM / THE WORLD OF MATTER / AND / THE WORLD OF
MAN. / BY / [red] THEODORE PARKER. / [rule] / SELECTED FROM NOTES
OF UNPUBLISHED / SERMONS, / BY RUFUS LEIGHTON. / [rule] / BOSTON: /
[red] PUBLISHED BY CHARLES W. SLACK. / 1865.

Pagination: [i–iv] v–xi [xii] [13–14] 15–430 [431–432].

Collation: [1]^8 2–27^8.

Contents: inserted leaf with engraving of Parker printed on verso;
p. 1: title page; p. 2: copyright information; p. iii: dedication
to Hannah Elizabeth Stevenson; p. iv: blank; pp. v–vi: 'PREFACE.'
dated 'WASHINGTON, D.C., May 10, 1865.'; pp. vii–xi: contents; p.
xii: blank; p. 13: 'LESSONS / FROM / THE WORLD OF MATTER / AND /
THE WORLD OF MAN.'; p. 14: eight lines of verse from Longfellow;
pp. 15–65: "The Material World and Man's Relation Thereto"; pp.
66–101: "The Nature of Man"; pp. 102–198: "Traits and Illustrations
of Human Character and Conduct"; pp. 199–212: "Phases of Domestic
Life"; pp. 213–250: "Education"; pp. 251–266: "Human Institutions
and National Life"; pp. 267–295: "The Power and Endurance of What
Is Noblest in Man"; pp. 296–314: "Human Progress"; pp. 315–337:
"Jesus of Nazareth"; pp. 338–430: "Man in His Religious Aspects";
pp. 431–432: blank.

Typography and paper: page size: 7 15/16" X 5 1/8"; text size:
6 1/8" (5 11/16") X 3 1/2"; laid paper with vertical chain lines
1 3/16" apart; 33 lines per page. Running heads: rectos: pp. ix–xi:
'CONTENTS.'; pp. 17–428: section titles; versos: p. vi: 'PREFACE.';
pp. viii–x: 'CONTENTS.'; pp. 16–430: section titles.

Binding: medium reddish brown; dark green C cloth (sand–grain);

bevelled edges; front and back covers: blindstamped triple-rule frame; spine: goldstamped '[rule] / [rule] / [rule] / LESSONS / FROM THE / WORLD OF MATTER / AND THE / WORLD OF MAN / by / THEODORE PARKER / [leaf design] / [gothic] Boston / [rule] / [rule] / [rule]'. Flyleaves. Yellow coated endpapers. All edges trimmed. Top edges gilded.

Printing: Unknown.

Publication: Inscribed copies: MB (rebound; from Rufus Leighton, 13 May 1865); CSt (from Rufus Leighton, May 1865); MH (rebound; 12 June 1865). MH-AH copy (rebound) received 30 June 1865. Price, $2.50.

Locations: CSt, JM, MB, MH-AH.

A 64.1.b
First edition, second printing (1871)

Title page: The same as in the first printing, except: '[red] LESSONS . . . BOSTON: / [red] PUBLISHED BY D. W. NILES, / 8 BROMFIELD STREET, / 1871.'.

430pp. Noted in *[Theodore Parker's Works]* binding (see B 2). Price, $1.50. *Location:* JM.

A 64.1.c
First edition, third printing (1873)

Title page: The same as in the first printing, except: 'LESSONS . . . BY / THEODORE . . . BOSTON: / JAMES CAMPBELL. / 1873.'.

430pp. *Location:* MdBP.

A 64.1.d
First edition, presumed fourth printing (1880)

Title page: The same as in the third printing, except: 'LESSONS

. . . BOSTON: / PUBLISHED BY N. R. CAMPBELL & CO. / 1880.'.

430pp. *Location:* PSt.

A 64.1.e
First edition, presumed fifth printing (1880)

Title page: The same as in the third printing, except: 'LESSONS
. . . LEIGHTON. / [rule] / CHICAGO: COLGROVE BOOK CO. / BOSTON: /
PUBLISHED BY N. R. CAMPBELL & CO. / 1880.'.

430pp. *Location:* MH–AH (rebound).

A 64.1.f
First edition, sixth printing (1886)

Title page: LESSONS / FROM / THE WORLD OF MATTER / AND / THE WORLD
OF MAN / BY / THEODORE PARKER / [gothic] Selected from Notes of
Unpublished Sermons / BY RUFUS LEIGHTON / CHICAGO / CHARLES H. KERR
AND COMPANY / 175 DEARBORN STREET / 1886'.

430pp. *Location:* MH–AH.

A 64.1.g
First edition, seventh printing (1887)

Title page: The same as in the third printing, except: 'LESSONS
. . . LEIGHTON. / [rule] / CHICAGO: / CHARLES H. KERR AND COMPANY, /
175 DEARBORN STREET. / 1887.'.

430pp. *Locations:* TxU, WaTC.

A 64.1.h
First edition, eighth printing (1892)

Title page: [initial display capital] LESSONS FROM THE WORLD OF /
MATTER AND THE WORLD OF / MAN: BY THEODORE PARKER.— / SELECTED

FROM NOTES OF UN- / PUBLISHED SERMONS: BY RUFUS / LEIGHTON. /
CHICAGO: / CHARLES H. KERR & COMPANY, / 1892.

430pp. Stiff wrappers. *Unity Library*, no. 16. Price, 50¢.
Location: JM.

A 64.1.i
First edition, ninth printing (1893)

Title page: The same as in the eighth printing, except: '[initial
display capital] LESSONS . . . COMPANY, / 1893.'.

430pp. Inscribed copy: JM (17 October 1893). *Location:* JM.

A 64.2.a
First English edition, first printing (1865)

LESSONS / FROM / THE WORLD OF MATTER / AND / THE WORLD OF MAN /
BY / THEODORE PARKER. / *SELECTED FROM NOTES OF UNPUBLISHED*
SERMONS, / BY RUFUS LEIGHTON. / EDITED BY / FRANCES POWER COBBE. /
LONDON: / TRÜBNER & CO., 60, PATERNOSTER ROW. / 1865. / *The right*
of reproduction and translation is reserved.

Pagination: [iii–vii] viii–xi [xii–xiii] xiv [xv] xvi–xix [xx] 1–41
[42] 43–70 [71] 72–147 [148] 149–158 [159] 160–188 [189] 190–201
[202] 203–224 [225] 226–239 [240] 241–258 [259] 260–331 [332–334].

Collation: $[a]^8{}_{(-a_1)}$ b^2 1–20^8 21^6 $[22]^2{}_{(-22_2)}$.

Contents: inserted leaf with engraving of Parker printed on verso;
p. iii: title page; p. iv: 12 lines of verse from Longfellow; p. v:
dedication; p. vi: blank; pp. vii–xi: 'PREFACE BY THE EDITOR.'
dated *'North Wales, Nov.* 1864.'; p. xii: blank; pp. xiii–xiv:
'PREFACE.' signed 'R. L. / *Washington, D.C., October*, 1864.'; pp.
xv–xix: contents; p. xx: blank; pp. 1–331: the same as in the first
edition; p. 332: blank; p. 333: 42 lines of errata; p. 334: blank.

Typography and paper: page size: 8" X 5 3/16"; text size: prefaces:
6 3/16" (5 15/16") X 3 1/2"; text: 6 1/4" (6") X 3 1/2"; wove paper;
prefaces: 38 lines per page; text: 22 lines per page. Running
heads: rectos and versos: section titles.

Binding: very dark red C cloth (sand-grain); bevelled edges; front
and back covers: blindstamped triple-rule frame; spine: goldstamped
'[band] / SELECTIONS / FROM / THEOD. / PARKER'S / UNPUBLISHED /
SERMONS. / [band] / [dotted triangle] / TRÜBNER & C? / [band]'.
Green coated endpapers. All edges trimmed.

Printing: John Childs and Son.

Publication: Deposit copy: BL (rebound; 3 February 1865). MBAt copy (rebound) received 25 February 1865. Inscribed copy: JM (19 May 1865). Price, 7s6d.

Locations: BE, JM.

A 64.2.b
First English edition, second printing (1871)

Title page: The same as in the first English edition, first printing, except: 'LESSONS . . . MAN. / BY . . . PARKER. / SELECTED FROM NOTES OF UNPUBLISHED SERMONS, / BY . . . LEIGHTON. / LONDON: . . . ROW. / 1871. / *The* . . .'.

331pp. *Collected Works*, vol. 14 (see B 1). Deposit copy: BL (27 January 1872). Price, 6s. *Locations:* BE, BL, BO.

A 64.2.c
First English edition, third printing (1872)

Title page: The same as in the first English edition, second printing, except: 'LESSONS . . . LEIGHTON. / [gothic] Third Edition. / LONDON: . . . ROW. / 1872. / *The* . . .'.

331pp. *Collected Works*, vol. 14 (see B 1). *Location:* JM.

A 64.3
Third edition, only printing [1908]

Title page: LESSONS FROM / THE WORLD OF MATTER AND / THE WORLD OF MAN / BY / THEODORE PARKER / EDITED WITH A PREFACE / BY / RUFUS LEIGHTON / [publisher's logo] / BOSTON / AMERICAN UNITARIAN ASSOCIATION / 25 BEACON STREET

419pp. *Centenary Edition*, vol. [5] (see B 3). MH–AH copy received 19 September 1910. Price, $1.00. *Locations:* InU, JM, MBAt, MH, MH–AH, NcU.

A 65   HISTORIC AMERICANS
         1870

A 65.1.a

First edition, first printing (1870)

HISTORIC AMERICANS. / BY / THEODORE PARKER. / [rule] / BOSTON: /
HORACE B. FULLER, / 14 BROMFIELD STREET. / 1870.

Pagination: [1–2] 3–9 [10] 11 [12–13] 14–73 [74] 75–147 [148]
149–231 [232] 233 [234] 235–295 [296] 297–312.

Collation: [1–13^{12}].   Signed [1]^8 2–19^8 [20]^4.

Contents: p. 1: title page; p. 2: copyright information and
printer's imprint; pp. 3–8: 'PREFACE.' signed 'O. B. F.'; p. 9:
contents; p. 10: blank; p. 11: 'FRANKLIN.'; p. 12: blank; pp. 13–72:
text; p. 73: 'WASHINGTON.'; p. 74: blank; pp. 75–146: text; p. 147:
'JOHN ADAMS.'; p. 148: blank; pp. 149–231: text; p. 232: blank; p.
233: 'THOMAS JEFFERSON.'; p. 234: blank; pp. 235–295: text; p. 296:
blank; pp. 297–312: index.

Typography and paper: page size: 4 7/8" X 8 1/2"; text size:
"Preface": 5 3/4" (5 3/8") X 3 3/8"; text: 5 3/4" (5 1/2") X 3 3/8";
wove paper; "Preface": 24 lines per page; text: 28 lines per page.
Running heads: rectos: pp. 5–7: 'PREFACE.'; pp. 15–295: chapter
titles; pp. 299–311: 'INDEX.'; versos: pp. 4–8: 'PREFACE.'; pp.
14–294: chapter titles; pp. 298–312: INDEX.'.

Binding: Two styles have been noted:

> *Binding A:* dark purple C cloth (sand-grain); front and back
> covers: blindstamped triple-rule frame with lines connecting
> the corners of the second and third frames, outside of a
> single-rule frame with intersecting lines in each corner;
> spine: goldstamped '[rule] / [rule] / HISTORIC AMERICANS /
> [rule] / THEODORE PARKER / [publisher's logo] / [rule] /

[rule]'. Flyleaves. Brown coated endpapers. All edges trimmed.

Binding B: the same as Binding A, except: spine: goldstamped: 'THEODORE PARKER'S / WORKS. / HISTORIC / AMERICANS / [publisher's logo]'. Undoubtedly a remainder binding; probably used for inclusion in *[Theodore Parker's Works]* (see B 2).

Printing: Stereotyped at the Boston Stereotype Foundry, 19 Spring Lane.

Publication: MBAt copy (rebound) received 16 November 1870. Inscribed copy: MH (from Lydia Parker, 7 December 1870). Price, $1.50.

Locations: Binding A: JM, MB; Binding B: MH.

Note one: A four-page undated catalogue of Fuller's publications, three pages of which are devoted to works by Parker, is inserted at the back.

Note two: Edited by Octavius Brooks Frothingham.

A 65.1.b
First edition, second printing (1871)

Title page: The same as in the first printing, except: 'HISTORIC . . . PARKER. / SECOND EDITION. / BOSTON: . . . STREET. / 1871.'.

312pp. Noted in *[Theodore Parker's Works]* binding (see B 2). Deposit copy: BL (25 April 1872). Price, $1.50. *Locations:* BL, JM, MH, MH-AH, ViU.

A 65.1.c
First edition, third printing (1878)

Title page: The same as in the first printing, except: 'HISTORIC
. . . FULLER, / 1878.'.

312pp. *Locations:* CSt, JM, MH.

A 65.2

First English edition, only printing (1871)

HISTORIC AMERICANS. / BY / THEODORE PARKER. / [rule] / LONDON: / TRÜBNER & CO., 60, PATERNOSTER ROW / 1871.

Pagination: [i–v] vi–viii [ix–x] [11–13] 14–57 [58–61] 62–114 [115–117] 118–178 [179–181] 182–226 [227] 228–236.

Collation: [1]^8 2–14^8 15^6.

Contents: p. i: *Collected Works* title page; p. ii: printer's imprint; p. iii: title page; p. iv: printer's imprint; pp. v–viii: "Preface"; p. ix: contents; p. x: blank; pp. 11–236: the same as in the first edition.

Typography and paper: page size: 8 13/16" X 5"; text size: "Preface": 6" (5 3/4") X 3 1/2"; text: 6 1/8" (5 13/16") X 3 1/2"; wove paper; "Preface": 32 lines per page; text: 35 lines per page. Running heads: rectos and versos: section titles.

Binding: very purplish blue L cloth (morocco); front and back covers: blindstamped single-rule frame, outside of a band with raised flower designs and lines connecting with the frame at each corner, outside of a single-rule frame; spine: goldstamped '[band] / [rule] / [rule] / [rule] / THEODORE / PARKER'S / WORKS / [rule] / VOL. XIII / HISTORIC / AMERICANS / TRÜBNER & C^O / [rule] / [rule] / [rule] / [band]'. Black coated endpapers. Top edges uncut; side and bottom edges trimmed.

Printing: John Childs and Son.

Publication: *Collected Works*, vol. 13 (see B 1). Price, 7s6d.

Locations: BE, BO, JM, MH, MH–AH.

Note: Also noted with a two-leaf preliminary gathering: p. i:
publisher's advertisement; p. ii: blank; p. iii: 'HISTORIC
AMERICANS.'; p. iv: blank. In *Collected Works* binding (see B 1)
with brown coated endpapers. Deposit copy: BL (27 January 1872).
Location: BL.

A 65.3
Third edition, only printing [1908]

Title page: HISTORIC AMERICANS / BY / THEODORE PARKER / EDITED WITH
NOTES / BY / SAMUEL A. ELIOT / [publisher's logo] / BOSTON /
AMERICAN UNITARIAN ASSOCIATION / 25 BEACON STREET

460pp. *Centenary Edition,* vol. [7] (see B 3). Copyright 6 January
1909. MH–AH copy received 24 September 1908. Price, $1.00.
Locations: InU, JM, MBAt, MH, MH–AH, NcU.

Note: Contains *Historic Americans;* "John Quincy Adams," see A 19;
"Daniel Webster," see A 31.

156

A 66   TRANSCENDENTALISM
           1876

A 66

First edition, only printing (1876)

FREE RELIGIOUS TRACTS. NO. 4. / [rule] / TRANSCENDENTALISM. / A
LECTURE BY / THEODORE PARKER. / [rule] / *NEVER BEFORE PRINTED.* /
[rule] / BOSTON: / PUBLISHED BY THE FREE RELIGIOUS ASSOCIATION, /
NO. 1 TREMONT PLACE. / 1876

Pagination: [1–3] 4 [5] 6–39 [40].

Collation: [1]^{20}.

Contents: p. 1: title page; p. 2: printer's imprint; pp. 3–4:
'PRELIMINARY NOTE.'; pp. 5–39: text; p. 40: publisher's
advertisement.

Typography and paper: page size: 7 5/8" X 4"; text size: 5 9/16" X
3 1/4"; wove paper; 35 lines per page. No running heads.

Binding: Cover title. All edges trimmed.

Printing: Cochrane and Sampson, 9 Bromfield Street, Boston.

Publication: Free Religious Tracts, no. 4. Price, 10¢.

Locations: JM, MH–AH, MHi.

A 67 THEODORE PARKER TO A YOUNG MAN
1885?

A 67.1
First edition, only printing [1885?]

THEODORE PARKER TO A YOUNG MAN. / [rule] / [Reprinted from the
Christian Register.* / [24 lines of text] / [two lines of
publication information]

Pagination: [1] 2-4.

Collation: Single leaf folded once to make four pages.

Contents: pp. 1-4: text.

Typography and paper: page size: 6 7/16" X 4 5/8"; text size:
5 5/8" X 3 1/2"; calendered paper; 36 lines per page. No running
heads.

Binding: Head title. All edges trimmed.

Printing: Christian Register Association, 141 Franklin Street,
Boston.

Publication: Price, 30¢ per hundred.

Locations: MB, MH-AH, MHi.

Note: Reprints Parker's letter of 7 July 1851 from the 23 July 1885
Christian Register.

A 67.2
Second edition, only printing [1899]

Title page: [gothic] Register Tract Series, No. 20.* / [rule] /
THEODORE PARKER TO A YOUNG / MAN.† / [rule] / [15 lines of text] /

[rule] / [three lines of publication information] / [three lines of printing history]

6pp. Head title. Published by the Christian Register Association, Boston. *Register Tract Series*, no. 20. Price, 50¢ per hundred. *Location:* MH–AH.

A 68   WEST ROXBURY SERMONS
          1892

A 68.1.a
First edition, first printing (1892)

WEST ROXBURY SERMONS / BY / THEODORE PARKER. / 1837–1848. / *FROM UNPUBLISHED MANUSCRIPTS.* / WITH / [gothic] Introduction and Biographical Sketch. / BOSTON: / ROBERTS BROTHERS. / 1892.

Pagination: [i–iv] [i–v] vi–xvi [xvii] xviii–xxiii [xxiv] [1] 2–14 [15] 16–29 [30] 31–44 [45] 46–57 [58] 59–71 [72] 73–88 [89] 90–104 [105] 106–118 [119] 120–129 [130] 131–144 [145] 146–160 [161] 162–177 [178] 179–196 [197] 198–215 [216] 217–235 [236–240].

Collation: [a]^8 [b]^6 1–15^8.

Contents: pp. i–ii: blank; p. iii: 'WEST ROXBURY SERMONS.'; p. iv: advertisement for Parker's *Prayers*; p. i: title page; p. ii: copyright information and printer's imprint; p. iii: contents; p. iv: blank; pp. v–xvi: 'INTRODUCTION.' signed 'SAMUEL J. BARROWS.'; pp. xvii–xxiii: 'BIOGRAPHICAL SKETCH.' signed 'F. B. SANBORN. / CONCORD. / *January* 24, 1892.'; p. xxiv: blank; pp. 1–14: "The Parable of the Talents"; pp. 15–29: "Spiritual Indifference"; pp. 30–44: "Tranquility"; pp. 45–57: "The World Belongs to Each Man"; pp. 58–71: "The Influence of Religion Upon the Feelings"; pp. 72–88: "The Application of Religion to Life"; pp. 89–104: "A Sermon of Man"; pp. 105–118: "The Fact of Life and the Idea of Life"; pp. 119–129: "The Crucifixion"; pp. 130–144: "Christian Advancement"; pp. 145–160: "Prayer and Intercourse with God"; pp. 161–177: "Christianity in Contrast with Heathenism"; pp. 178–196: "Low Aims and Lofty"; pp. 197–215: "God's Income to Man"; pp. 216–235: "The Doctrine of Inspiration"; p. 236: blank; pp. 237–240: publisher's advertisements.

Typography and paper: page size: 7 11/16" X 4 1/2"; text size: introductions: 5 1/2" (5 3/16") X 3 1/8"; text: 5 1/2" (5 1/8") X

3 1/8"; wove paper; introductions: 30 lines per page; text: 28 lines per page. Running heads: rectos and versos: chapter titles.

Binding: dark brown; gray olive green BF cloth (fine bead-grain); front cover: goldstamped in the upper left corner, each line to the right of the line above: 'WEST / ROXBURY / SERMONS'; back cover: blank; spine: goldstamped 'WEST / ROXBURY / SERMONS / THEODORE / PARKER / [two lines in hand-lettering] BOSTON / ROBERTS BROS.'. Dark grayish blue coated endpapers. All edges trimmed.

Printing: John Wilson and Son, University Press, Cambridge.

Publication: 500 copies printed on 10 March 1892. Copyright, 21-26 March 1892. Deposit copy: BL (30 June 1892). MH-AH copy received 13 April 1892. Inscribed copy: JM (14 April 1892). Listed in the *English Catalogue* as an importation in April 1892 at 5s. Price, $1.00. A royalty of 10% of the retail price on each copy sold was to be paid F. B. Sanborn on account with S. J. Barrows.

Locations: BL, JM, MH-AH.

A 68.1.b
First edition, second printing (1902)

Title page: West Roxbury Sermons / By / Theodore Parker / 1837-1848 / *From Unpublished Manuscripts* / With Introduction and / Biographical Sketch / Boston / American Unitarian Association / 1902

235pp. Price, 75¢. *Locations:* JM, MBAt.

SECTION B:
COLLECTED EDITIONS

B 1   THE COLLECTED WORKS OF THEODORE PARKER
1863-1871

The Collected Works of Theodore Parker, 14 vols. Edited by Frances
Power Cobbe. London: Trübner & Co., 1863-1871. Some volumes also
noted with N. Trübner & Co. imprint.

Works title page. Page size: 8 13/16" X 5". Printed by John Childs
and Son, London. Binding of very purplish blue L cloth (morocco);
for further information, see A 65.2. Price, 6s per volume.

1.   *A Discourse of Matters Pertaining to Religion* (1863).
        Reprinted 1872, 1876. See A 4.7.a, A 4.7.c.

2   *Ten Sermons of Religion* (1863). Reprinted 1879. See A 32.3.

3   *Discourses of Theology* (1863). Reprinted 1875. See C 6.

4   *Discourses of Politics* (1863). See C 7.

5-6   *Discourses of Slavery*, 2 vols. (1863). See C 9.

7   *Discourses of Social Science* (1864). See C 10.

8   *Miscellaneous Discourses* (1864). See C 11.

9-10   *Critical Writings*, 2 vols. (1864-1865). See C 12.

11   *Sermons of Theism, Atheism, and the Popular Theology* (1865).
        Reprinted 1867. See A 36.4.

12   *Autobiographical and Miscellaneous Pieces* (1865). See C 13.

13   *Historic Americans* (1871). See A 65.2.

14   *Lessons from the World of Matter and the World of Man* (1871).
        Reprinted 1872. See A 64.2.b-c.

B 2   [THEODORE PARKER'S WORKS]
       1864-1871

[Theodore Parker's Works], 10 vols. Two imprints noted: New York:
D. Appleton & Co.; Boston: T. O. H. P. Burnham, 1864; and Boston:
Horace B. Fuller, 1867-1871.

No *Works* half title. Identified as a *Works* edition on the spine
stamping. Page sizes: 8 7/8" X 5" (1864); 8 5/16" X 5" (1867-1871).
Bindings of black T cloth (rib), with 'THEODORE PARKER'S / WORKS'
and the title goldstamped on the spine; and dark grayish red C cloth
(sand-grain), with goldstamped 'THEODORE PARKER'S / WORKS', title,
and publisher's logo on the spine; for cover blindstamping on both
bindings, see A 45.1.a, Binding B. Copies have been noted with
mixed sheets and casings. Prices: $1.50 per volume; advertised as
late as 1878 as "bound in uniform style" and "in a neat box" at
$15.00 the set. The order of the volumes is arbitrary.

1   *A Discourse of Matters Pertaining to Religion* (1864).
        Reprinted 1870. See A 4.6.b–c.
2   *Sermons of Theism, Atheism, and the Popular Theology* (1864).
        Reprinted 1870. See A 36.3.c–d.
3   *Ten Sermons of Religion* (1864). See A 32.1.d.
4–6   *Speeches, Addresses, and Occasional Sermons*, 3 vols. (1864).
        Reprinted 1867, 1871. See A 29.2.b–d.
7–8   *Additional Speeches, Addresses, and Occasional Sermons*, 2
        vols. (1864). Reprinted 1867. See A 45.1.c–d.
9   *Critical and Miscellaneous Writings* (1864). Reprinted 1867,
        [1870]. See A 6.3.c–e.
10   *Historic Americans* (1870). Reprinted 1871. See A 65.1.a–b.

Note: A copy of *Lessons from the World of Matter and the World of
Man* has been noted in a *Works* binding, probably a remaindered copy
since this title was not advertised as part of the *Works* set; for
further information, see A 64.1.b.

B 3   CENTENARY EDITION
1907-1912

Centenary Edition, 15 vols.   Boston: American Unitarian Association,
[1907-1912].

Identified as the *Centenary Edition* on the half title.   Page size:
8 1/8" X 5 1/8".   Printed by the University Press, Cambridge.
Primary binding of grayish olive green S cloth (diagonal fine-rib),
with goldstamped: all within a single-rule frame: '[title] /
[rule] / THEODORE / PARKER / [design] / CENTENARY / EDITION /
[leaf-and-vine design]' on the spine, and goldstamped ornate 'TP'
within a single-rule frame on the front cover.   Top edges gilded.
Also noted in dark yellow green B cloth (linen), with goldstamped
'[rule] / [title] / [rule] / THEODORE / PARKER / [rule]' on the
spine, and blindstamped: all within a triple-rule frame: '[title] /
[rule] / [winged ornament] / [rule] / THEODORE PARKER' on the front
cover (possibly a binding for English sale; the only located copies
have the library stamp of the British and Foreign Unitarian
Association [JM]).   Prices: $1.00 per volume; $10.00 the set.   The
order of the volumes is taken from the listing in the "Bibliography"
in vol. 15.

1   *A Discourse of Matters Pertaining to Religion*, ed. Thomas
        Wentworth Higginson [1907].   See A 4.9.
2   *Sermons of Theism, Atheism, and the Popular Theology*, ed.
        Charles W. Wendte [1907].   See A 36.5.
3   *Sermons of Religion*, ed. Samuel A. Eliot [1908].   See C 41.
4   *The Transient and Permanent in Christianity*, ed. George
        Willis Cooke [1908].   See C 40.
5   *Lessons from the World of Matter and the World of Man*, ed.
        Rufus Leighton [1908].   See A 64.3.
6   *The World of Matter and the Spirit of Man*, ed. George Willis
        Cooke [1907].   See C 38.
7   *Historic Americans*, ed. Samuel A. Eliot [1908].   See A 65.3.
8   *The American Scholar*, ed. George Willis Cooke [1907].   See
        C 39.

9   *Sins and Safeguards of Society*, ed. Samuel B. Stewart [1909].
     See C 42.

10   *Social Classes in a Republic*, ed. Samuel A. Eliot [1910].
     See C 43.

11   *The Slave Power*, ed. James K. Hosmer [1910]. See C 44.

12   *The Rights of Man in America*, ed. F. B. Sanborn [1911].
     See C 45.

13   *Autobiography, Poems, and Prayers*, ed. Rufus Leighton
     [1911?]. See C 46.

14   *Saint Bernard and Other Papers*, ed. Charles W. Wendte
     [1911]. See C 47.

15   *Bibliography and Index* [1912]. 166pp. Contains Thomas
     Wentworth Higginson, "The Parker Library" (reprinted from
     *Thirty-First Annual Report of the Trustees of the
     [Boston] Public Library* [Boston: n.p., 1883], pp. 19–25);
     "Bibliography" by Charles W. Wendte; and "Index" by
     Arthur A. Brooks.

SECTION C:
COLLECTIONS AND SELECTIONS

C 1   THE BIBLE
[1851?]

First printing [1851?]: No. 1—TRACTS FOR THE TIMES. / [rule] / THE
BIBLE: / WHAT IT IS, AND WHAT IT IS NOT. / BY THEODORE PARKER, /
MINISTER OF THE SECOND CHURCH IN ROXBURY, MASS. / [rule] / [33 lines
of text]

16pp. Head title. Published by John Robertson, Glasgow. Reprinted
from *A Discourse of Matters Pertaining to Religion* (A 4), pp. 317–
377. *Tracts for the Times*, no. 1. Advertised for sale in *The
People*, n.s. 2 (31 January 1852): 40. Price, 2d. *Location:* NN.

Second printing [1852?]: The title page is the same as in the first
printing, except: '[SECOND EDITION.] / [ornate rule] / No. . . .
SECOND CONGREGATIONAL CHURCH / IN . . . [rule] / [33 lines of
text]'.

16pp. Head title. Published by John Robertson, Glasgow.
Location: NN.

C 2   CHRISTIANITY
[1851?]

Fourth printing [1852?]: FOURTH THOUSAND. / [rule] / No. 2.—TRACTS
FOR THE TIMES. / [rule] / CHRISTIANITY: / WHAT IT IS, AND WHAT IT
IS NOT. / BY THEODORE PARKER, / MINISTER OF THE SECOND CHURCH,
ROXBURY, MASS. / [rule] / [34 lines of text]

20pp. Head title. Published by John Robertson, Glasgow. Reprinted
from *A Discourse of Matters Pertaining to Religion* (A 4), pp. 237–
314. *Tracts for the Times*, no. 2. Advertised for sale in *The
People*, n.s. 2 (31 January 1852): 40. Price, 2d. *Location:* NN.

Note: No copies earlier than the fourth thousand have been located.

Fifth printing [1852?]: The title page is the same as in the fourth printing, except: *'FIFTH THOUSAND. . . .* [34 lines of text]'.

20pp. Head title. Published by John Robertson, Glasgow. *Location:* NN.

C 3   STRAUSS'S LIFE OF JESUS
         [1852]

Only printing [1852]: TRACTS FOR THE TIMES—No. 8. / [rule] / STRAUSS'S LIFE OF JESUS, / EXAMINED BY / THEODORE PARKER, / MINISTER OF THE TWENTY-SECOND CONGREGATIONAL CHURCH, / BOSTON, MASS. / [rule] / [33 lines of text]

16pp. Head title. Published by John Robertson, Glasgow. *Tracts for the Times,* no. 8. Published July 1852. Price, 2d. *Location:* NN.

Note one: For first book publication, see A 5; for publication of the second part of Strauss, see C 4.

Note two: Parker was minister of the Twenty-Eighth, not the Twenty-Second, Congregational Society.

C 4   THE RELIGIOUS SENTIMENT
         [1852]

Only printing [1852]: TRACTS FOR THE TIMES—No. 9. / [rule] / THE RELIGIOUS SENTIMENT: / ITS INFLUENCE ON LIFE. / BY / THEODORE PARKER, / MINISTER OF THE TWENTY-SECOND CONGREGATIONAL CHURCH, / BOSTON, MASS. / [rule] / [34 lines of text]

14pp. Head title. Published by John Robertson, Glasgow. Contains "The Religious Sentiment" and "Strauss's Life of Jesus." *Tracts for the Times,* no. 9. Published October 1852. Price, 2d. *Location:* NN.

Note one: See *A Discourse of Matters Pertaining to Religion* (A 4), pp. 132–155, and for the first book publication of Strauss, see A 5; for publication of the first part of Strauss, see C 3.

Note two: Parker was minister of the Twenty-Eighth, not the Twenty-Second, Congregational Society.

C 5   LIFE AND CORRESPONDENCE OF THEODORE PARKER
1863

First printing (1863): LIFE AND CORRESPONDENCE / OF / THEODORE PARKER, / MINISTER OF THE / TWENTY-EIGHTH CONGREGATIONAL SOCIETY, BOSTON. / BY / JOHN WEISS. / IN TWO VOLUMES. / VOL. I. [II.] / LONDON: / LONGMAN, GREEN, LONGMAN, ROBERTS, AND GREEN. / 1863.

478pp., 529pp. Contains numerous letters and journal entries, and all of *Theodore Parker's Experience as a Minister* (A 58). Deposit copy: BL (20 February 1864). Price, 30s the set. *Locations:* BL, JM.

Second printing (1864): The title page is the same as in the first printing, except: 'LIFE . . . [II.] / NEW YORK: / D. APPLETON & CO., 443 & 445 BROADWAY / 1864.'.

478pp., 529pp. Price, $6.00 the set. *Locations:* JM, MB.

Third printing (1969): Freeport, N.Y.: Books for Libraries Press, 1969. *Location:* DLC (deposit copy, 4 February 1969).

Fourth printing (1969): New York: Bergman, 1969. Price, $42.50. *Location:* DLC (deposit copy, 8 September 1969).

Fifth printing (1969): New York: Negro Universities Press, 1969. Price, $31.00. *Location:* DLC (deposit copy, 15 May 1970).

Sixth printing (1969): New York: Arno Press, 1969. Price, $35.00. *Location:* DLC (deposit copy, 24 June 1970).

Seventh printing (1970): New York: Da Capo Press, 1970. Price,
$42.50. *Location:* DLC (deposit copy, 3 June 1970).

C 6   DISCOURSES OF THEOLOGY
1863

Presumed first printing (1863): DISCOURSES / OF / THEOLOGY. / BY /
THEODORE PARKER. / LONDON: / TRÜBNER & CO., 60, PATERNOSTER ROW. /
1863.

319pp. *Collected Works,* vol. 3 (see B 1). Deposit copy: BL (14
July 1863). Price, 6s. *Locations:* BL, BO.

Contents and printing histories: "The Relation of Jesus to His Age
and the Ages," see A 8; "A Sermon of Immortal Life," see A 14; "The
Idea of a Christian Church," see A 11; "Some Thoughts on the Most
Christian Use of the Sunday," see A 18; "A Sermon of Old Age," see
A 37; "A Discourse of the Function of a Teacher of Religion in These
Times," see A 46; "On the Delights of Piety. A Sermon Delivered at
the Opening Session of the Yearly Meeting of Progressive Friends,
Held at Longwood (Near Kennett Square), Chester County,
Pennsylvania, on Sunday, May 20, 1855," *Proceedings of the
Pennsylvania Yearly Meeting of Progressive Friends, Held at
Longwood, Near Kennett Square, Chester County, Fifth Month, 1855*
(New York: John F. Trow, 1855), pp. 41-54; "A Discourse of the
Relation Between the Ecclesiastical Instruction and the Religious
Consciousness of the American People. Delivered at the Opening of
the Progressive Friends' Meeting-House, at Longwood, Chester County,
Pennsylvania, May 19, 1855," *Proceedings of the Yearly Meeting of
Progressive Friends,* pp. 59-96; "A False and True Revival of
Religion," see A 52; "The Revival of Religion Which We Need," see
A 53; "False and True Theology," see A 51; "Beauty in the World of
Matter, Considered as a Revelation of God," see A 57; "What Religion
May Do for a Man," see A 59; "Farewell Letter, to the Members of the
Twenty-Eighth Congregational Society in Boston," see A 58.

Presumed second printing (1863): THE / COLLECTED WORKS / OF /
THEODORE PARKER, / MINISTER OF THE TWENTY-EIGHTH CONGREGATIONAL /
SOCIETY AT BOSTON, U.S. / CONTAINING HIS / THEOLOGICAL, POLEMICAL,
AND CRITICAL WRITINGS, / SERMONS, SPEECHES, AND ADDRESSES, / AND
LITERARY MISCELLANIES. / EDITED BY / FRANCES POWER COBBE. / VOL.
III. / DISCOURSES OF THEOLOGY. / LONDON: / TRÜBNER & CO., 60,
PATERNOSTER ROW. / 1863.

319pp. *Collected Works*, vol. 3 (see B 1). *Locations:* BE, MH-AH,
NcU.

Third printing (1875): The title page is the same as in the first
printing, except: 'DISCOURSES . . . CO., 57 & 59, LUDGATE HILL. /
1875.'.

319pp. *Collected Works*, vol. 3 (see B 1). *Location:* JM.

C 7   DISCOURSES OF POLITICS
1863

First printing (1863): DISCOURSES / OF / POLITICS. / BY / THEODORE
PARKER, / MINISTER OF THE TWENTY-EIGHTH CONGREGATIONAL CHURCH IN
BOSTON. / LONDON: / TRÜBNER & CO., 60, PATERNOSTER ROW. / 1863.

311pp. *Collected Works*, vol. 4 (see B 1). Deposit copy: BL (14
July 1863). Price, 6s. *Locations:* BE, BL, BO, JM, MH-AH, NcU.

Contents and printing histories: "A Sermon of War," see A 12;
"Speech Delivered at the Anti-War Meeting, in Faneuil Hall, February
4, 1847," see A 29; "A Sermon of the Mexican War," see A 20; "The
Political Destination of America and the Signs of the Times.
Delivered Before Several Literary Societies, 1848," see A 29; "Some
Thoughts on the Free Soil Party and the Election of General Taylor,
December, 1848," see A 29; "A Discourse Occasioned by the Death of
John Quincy Adams," see A 19; "A Discourse Occasioned by the Death
of the Late President Taylor. Preached at the Melodeon, July 14,
1850," see A 29; "Theodore Parker's Review of Webster," see A 23;

"The State of the Nation," see A 25; "The Aspect of Freedom in America. A Speech at the Massachusetts Anti-Slavery Celebration of Independence, at Abington, July 5, 1852," see A 45; "A New Lesson for the Day," see A 49.

Second (partial) printing (1973): Sermons on War by Theodore Parker / comprising / *A Sermon of War* / *Speech Delivered at the Anti-War Meeting* / *A Sermon of the Mexican War* / from *The Collected Works of Theodore Parker*, / Edited by Frances P. Cobbe / with a new introduction / for the Garland Edition *by* / Alice Kessler Harris / [publisher's logo] / *Garland Publishing, Inc., New York & London* / *1973*

76pp. Deposit copy: DLC (16 August 1973). Price, $6.50. *Location:* DLC.

C 8   THE WORKS OF THEODORE PARKER
1863

Only printing (1863): THE WORKS / OF / THEODORE PARKER, / MINISTER OF THE TWENTY-EIGHTH CONGREGATIONAL / CHURCH, BOSTON, U.S. / [rule] / IN EIGHT VOLUMES. / [rule] / VOLUME I. / [rule] / LONDON: / BARKER & CO., 4, THANET PLACE, TEMPLE BAR, STRAND. / [rule] / 1863.

210pp. Wrappers. Deposit copy: BL (17 September 1863). Price, 2s. *Location:* BL.

Contents and printing histories: "A Sermon of the Moral Condition of Boston," see A 21; "The Relation of Jesus to His Age and the Ages," see A 8; "The True Idea of a Christian Church," see A 11; "Some Thoughts on the Most Christian Use of the Sunday," see A 18; "A Sermon of Poverty," see A 29; "A Sermon of the Perishing Classes in Boston," see A 13; "A Sermon of Merchants," see A 15; "A Discourse of the Function of a Teacher of Religion in These Times," see A 46; "A Sermon of the Dangerous Classes in Society," see A 16; "The State of the Nation, Considered in a Sermon for Thanksgiving Day," see A 25.

Note: "We announced at first our intention of publishing the whole of Mr. Parker's Works in Eight Volumes, at 1s. 6d. per Volume to Subscribers, provided we could get 1,000 Subscribers guaranteed. We are sorry to say, that *we have not* received one third the number. We have consequently given up the idea of publishing them at that Price. . . . [Instead] we have decided to try and issue our Edition . . . at 2s. a Volume, *without* a guaranteed list of Subscribers,— and as we are not able to run the risk of publishing the whole at once, we shall issue One Volume at a time" (p. 1). Apparently no more volumes were published.

C 9   DISCOURSES OF SLAVERY
1863-1864

Only printing (1863): DISCOURSES / OF / SLAVERY. / BY / THEODORE PARKER. / [VOL. II. /] LONDON: / TRÜBNER & CO., 60 PATERNOSTER ROW. / 1863. [1864.]

328pp., 323pp. "Preface" by Frances Power Cobbe. *Collected Works*, vols. 5-6 (see B 1). Desposit copies: vol. 1: BL (29 October 1863); vol. 2: BL (26 April 1864). *Locations:* BE, BL, BO, JM, MH-AH, NcU.

Contents and printing histories: vol. 1: "A Sermon of Slavery," see A 7; "A Letter to the People of the United States Touching the Matter of Slavery," see A 17; "Speech at a Meeting of the American Anti-Slavery Society, to Celebrate the Abolition of Slavery by the French Republic, April 6, 1848," see A 29; "Speech at Faneuil Hall, Before the New England Anti-Slavery Convention, May 31, 1848," see A 29; "Speech at the New England Anti-Slavery Convention in Boston, May 29, 1850," see A 29; "The Function and Place of Conscience, in Relation to the Laws of Men," see A 24; "Speech at the Ministerial Conference in Boston, May 29, 1851," see A 45; "The Boston Kidnapping," see A 30; "The Law of God and the Statutes of Men," see A 41; "The Nebraska Question," see A 38; "An Address Delivered on the Condition of Man . . . Before the New York City Anti-Slavery Society . . . May 12, 1854," see A 39; vol. 2: "Some Thoughts on the Progress of America, and the Influence of Her Diverse Institutions.

An Address Prepared for the Anti-Slavery Convention in Boston, May
31, 1854," see A 45; "The New Crime Against Humanity," see A 40;
"A Sermon of the Dangers Which Threaten the Rights of Man in
America," see A 42; "An Address Delivered . . . Before the New York
City Anti-Slavery Society . . . May 12, 1854," see A 39; "A Sermon
of the Consequences of an Immoral Principle and False Idea of
Life," see A 44; "The Great Battle Between Slavery and Freedom,"
see A 48; "The Present Crisis in American Affairs: The
Slave-Holders' Attempt to Wrench the Territories from the Working
People, and to Spread Bondage Over All the Land, Delivered on the
Evening of May 7 [1856]," see A 48; "The Present Aspect of Slavery
in America," see A 50.

C 10   DISCOURSES OF SOCIAL SCIENCE
1864

Only printing (1864): DISCOURSES / OF / SOCIAL SCIENCE. / BY /
THEODORE PARKER. / LONDON: / TRÜBNER & CO., 60, PATERNOSTER ROW. /
1864.

295pp. *Collected Works*, vol. 7 (see B 1). Deposit copy: BL (7
March 1864). Price, 6s. *Locations:* BE, BL, BO, JM, MH-AH, NcU.

Contents and printing histories: "A Sermon of Merchants," see A 15;
"A Sermon of the Perishing Classes in Boston," see A 13; "A Sermon
of the Dangerous Classes in Society," see A 16; "A Sermon of
Poverty," see A 29; "A Sermon of the Moral Condition of Boston,"
see A 21; "A Sermon of the Spiritual Condition of Boston," see A 21;
"The Public Education of the People," see A 22; "The Position and
Duties of the American Scholar," see A 29; "The Chief Sins of the
People," see A 26.

C 11   MISCELLANEOUS DISCOURSES
1864

Only printing (1864): MISCELLANEOUS / DISCOURSES. / BY / THEODORE
PARKER. / LONDON: / TRÜBNER & CO., 60 PATERNOSTER ROW. / 1864.

219pp. *Collected Works*, vol. 8 (see B 1). Deposit copy: BL (30
June 1864). Price, 6s. *Locations:* BE, BL, BO, JM, MH-AH, NcU.

Contents and printing histories: "A Discourse on the Transient and
Permanent in Christianity," see A 2; "On the Education of the
Labouring Classes," see A 3; "The Three Chief Safeguards of
Society," see A 28; "A Sermon of the Public Function of Woman,"
see A 34; "A Sermon of the Moral Dangers Incident to Prosperity,"
see A 43; "The Effect of Slavery on the American People," see A 56;
"The Material Condition of the People of Massachusetts," see A 62;
The Two Christmas Celebrations, see A 60.

C 12 CRITICAL WRITINGS
1864-1865

Only printing (1864): CRITICAL WRITINGS. / BY / THEODORE PARKER. /
VOL. I. [II.] / LONDON: / TRÜBNER & CO., 60, PATERNOSTER ROW. /
1864. [1865.]

292pp., 308pp. *Collected Works*, vols. 9-10. Deposit copies: vol.
1: BL (17 October 1864); vol. 2: BL (18 October 1870). Price, 12s
the set. *Locations:* BE, BL, BO, JM, MH-AH, NcU.

Contents and printing histories: vol. 1: "A Lesson for the Day," see
A 6; "Truth Against the World," see A 6; "Strauss's Life of Jesus,"
see A 6; "The Life of St. Bernard of Clairvaux," see A 6; "Thoughts
on Labor," see A 6; "The Pharisees," see A 6; "How to Move the
World," see A 6; "German Literature," see A 6; "Primitive
Christianity," see A 6; "Thoughts on Theology," see A 6; "The
Excellence of Goodness," see A 9; "Education of the People," see
A 22; vol. 2: "The Hebrew Monarchy," *Massachusetts Quarterly Review*,
1 (March 1848): 225-239; "Ballad Literature," *Massachusetts
Quarterly Review*, 1 (March 1848): 240-255; "William Ellery
Channing," *Massachusetts Quarterly Review*, 1 (September 1848): 423-
456; "The Eternity of God," *Massachusetts Quarterly Review*, 2
(March 1849): 183-188; "Sonnets": "Jesus There is No Name So Dear

as Thine," *Liberty Bell* (Boston: Massachusetts Anti-Slavery Fair, 1846), pp. 54–55; "Oh Thou Great Friend to All the Sons of Men," *Liberty Bell*, pp. 55–56; "Dear Jesus Were Thy Spirit Now on Earth," *Liberty Bell*, pp. 56–57; "A Sonnet for the Times," *Liberty Bell* (Boston: Massachusetts Anti-Slavery Fair, 1851), p. 147; "Character of Mr. Prescott as an Historian," *Massachusetts Quarterly Review*, 2 (March 1849): 215–248; "Prescott's Conquest of Mexico," *Massachusetts Quarterly Review*, 2 (September 1849): 437–470; "The Administration of the Late Mr. Polk," *Massachusetts Quarterly Review*, 3 (December 1849): 118–157; "The Writings of Ralph Waldo Emerson," *Massachusetts Quarterly Review*, 3 (March 1850): 200–255; "Hildreth's History of the United States," *Massachusetts Quarterly Review*, 3 (June 1850): 386–425; "Some Thoughts on the Different Opinions of the New Testament Relative to the Personality of Jesus," *Massachusetts Quarterly Review*, 3 (September 1850): 512–523.

C 13   AUTOBIOGRAPHICAL AND MISCELLANEOUS PIECES 1865

Only printing (1865): AUTOBIOGRAPHICAL / AND / MISCELLANEOUS PIECES. / BY / THEODORE PARKER. / LONDON: / TRÜBNER & CO., 60, PATERNOSTER ROW. / 1865.

356pp. *Collected Works*, vol. 12 (see B 1). Deposit copy: BL (8 March 1865). Price, 6s. *Locations:* BE, BL, BO, JM, MH-AH, NcU.

Contents and printing histories: "The Like and the Different," *Liberty Bell* (Boston: Massachusetts Anti-Slavery Fair, 1852), pp. 122–140; "A Discourse Occasioned by the Death of Daniel Webster," see A 31; "Buckle's History of Civilization," *Christian Examiner*, 64 (March 1858): 233–276; "A Bumblebee's Thoughts on the Plan and Purpose of the Universe," E. Desor, "Esquiesse de la vie de Theodore Parker," *Album von Combe-Varin. Zur Errinerung an Theodore Parker und Hans Lorenz Küchler*, ed. Mayer von Esslingen (Zurich: Schabelitz'sche Buchhandlung, 1861), pp. 309–331; "John Brown's Expedition," see A 61; "A Letter to the Boston Association of Congregational Ministers," see A 10; "Two Sermons Preached Before

the Twenty-Eighth Congregational Society," see A 33; "A Friendly
Letter to the Executive Committee of the American Unitarian
Association," see A 35; *Theodore Parker's Experience as a Minister*,
see A 58.

C 14-C 28   GLEANINGS FROM THEODORE PARKER'S WORKS
1871-1872
The order of numbers is arbitrary.

C 14   HEBRAISM, HEATHENISM, BARBARISM
1871

Only printing (1871): GLEANINGS / FROM / THEODORE PARKER'S WORKS, /
WITH ADDITIONS. / HEBRAISM, HEATHENISM, BARBARISM, / SELECTED,
PREPARED AND PUBLISHED / BY / ROSS WINANS. / [wavy rule] /
BALTIMORE: / JOHN P. DES FORGES. / 1871.

15pp. Cover title. *Locations:* MB, NN, ViU.

C 15   NATURAL RELIGION, ATHEISM, AND POPULAR THEOLOGY
1871

Only printing (1871): GLEANINGS / FROM / THEODORE PARKER'S WORKS, /
WITH ADDITIONS. / NATURAL RELIGION, ATHEISM, AND POPULAR THEOLOGY. /
SELECTED, PREPARED AND PUBLISHED / BY / ROSS WINANS. / [rule] /
BALTIMORE: / JOHN P. DES FORGES. / 1871.

25pp. Cover title. *Locations:* MB, MH, NN, ViU.

C 16   SPECULATIVE THEISM
1871

Only printing (1871): GLEANINGS / FROM / THEODORE PARKER'S WORKS /
ON / SPECULATIVE THEISM. / SELECTED AND PUBLISHED / BY / ROSS
WINANS. / [rule] / BALTIMORE: / JOHN P. DES FORGES. / 1871.

19pp. Cover title. *Locations:* MB, NN.

C 17 PRACTICAL THEISM
1871

Only printing (1871): GLEANINGS / FROM / THEODORE PARKER'S WORKS / ON / PRACTICAL THEISM. / SELECTED AND PUBLISHED / BY / ROSS WINANS. / [rule] / BALTIMORE: / JOHN P. DES FORGES. / 1871.

16pp. Cover title. *Locations:* MB, NN, ViU.

C 18 REMARKS ABOUT JESUS
1872

Only printing (1872): GLEANINGS / FROM / THEODORE PARKER'S WORKS, / WITH ADDITIONS. / REMARKS ABOUT JESUS. / SELECTED, PREPARED AND PUBLISHED / BY / ROSS WINANS. / [rule] / BALTIMORE: / JOHN P. DES FORGES. / 1872.

8pp. Cover title. *Locations:* MB, NN, ViU.

C 19 CHRIST HAD NO CREED
1872

Only printing (1872): [all within a double-rule frame forming a ribbon design] GLEANINGS / FROM / THEODORE PARKER'S WORKS, / WITH ADDITIONS. / CHRIST HAD NO CREED. / SELECTED, PREPARED AND PUBLISHED / BY / ROSS WINANS. / [rule] / BALTIMORE: / JOHN P. DES FORGES. / 1872.

11pp. Cover title. *Locations:* MB, NN, ViU.

C 20 UNIVERSAL PROVIDENCE OF GOD
1872

Only printing (1872): GLEANINGS / FROM / THEODORE PARKER'S WORKS. / UNIVERSAL PROVIDENCE OF GOD. / SELECTED, PREPARED AND PUBLISHED / BY / ROSS WINANS. / [rule] / BALTIMORE: / JOHN P. DES FORGES. / 1872.

16pp. Cover title. *Locations:* MB, NN, ViU.

C 21   THE INFLUENCE OF THE RELIGIOUS ELEMENT ON LIFE
         1872

Only printing (1872): GLEANINGS / FROM / THEODORE PARKER'S WORKS, /
WITH ADDITIONS, / THE INFLUENCE OF THE RELIGIOUS ELEMENT / ON
LIFE. / SELECTED, PREPARED AND PUBLISHED / BY / ROSS WINANS. /
[rule] / BALTIMORE: / JOHN P. DES FORGES. / 1872.

16pp. Wrappers. *Locations:* MB, NN, ViU.

C 22   THEISM AND ATHEISM
         1872

Only printing (1872): GLEANINGS / FROM / THEODORE PARKER'S WORKS, /
WITH ADDITIONS, / THEISM AND ATHEISM. / SELECTED, PREPARED AND
PUBLISHED / BY / ROSS WINANS. / [rule] / BALTIMORE: / JOHN P. DES
FORGES. / 1872.

18pp. Wrappers. *Locations:* MB, NN, ViU.

C 23   IMMORTALITY IS A FACT OF MAN'S NATURE
         1872

Only printing (1872): GLEANINGS / Condensed from Parker's Works. /
[rule] / IMMORTALITY IS A FACT OF MAN'S NATURE. / [rule] / SELECTED,
PREPARED AND PUBLISHED / BY / ROSS WINANS. / [rule] / BALTIMORE: /
JOHN P. DES FORGES. / 1872.

15pp. Cover title. *Locations:* MB, NN, ViU.

C 24   A MAN IS EDUCATED BECAUSE HE IS A MAN
         1872

Only printing (1872): GLEANINGS / Condensed from Parker's Works. /
[rule] / A MAN IS EDUCATED BECAUSE HE IS A MAN. / [rule] / SELECTED,

PREPARED AND PUBLISHED / BY / ROSS WINANS. / [rule] / BALTIMORE: /
JOHN P. DES FORGES. / 1872.

26pp. Cover title. *Locations:* MB, NN, ViU.

C 25   THOUGHTS ON LABOR
         1872

Only printing (1872): GLEANINGS / FROM / THEODORE PARKER'S WORKS, /
WITH ADDITIONS. / [rule] / THOUGHTS ON LABOR. / SELECTED, PREPARED
AND PUBLISHED / BY / ROSS WINANS. / [rule] / BALTIMORE: / JOHN P.
DES FORGES. / 1872.

22pp. Cover title. *Locations:* MB, NN, ViU.

C 26   THE RELATION OF THE RELIGIOUS SENTIMENT TO GOD; OR, A
         DISCOURSE OF INSPIRATION
         1872

Only printing (1872): GLEANINGS / FROM / THEODORE PARKER'S WORKS, /
WITH ADDITIONS. / THE RELATION OF THE RELIGIOUS SENTIMENT TO GOD; /
OR, / A DISCOURSE OF INSPIRATION. / SELECTED, PREPARED AND
PUBLISHED / BY / ROSS WINANS. / [rule] / BALTIMORE: / JOHN P. DES
FORGES. / 1872.

27pp. Cover title. *Locations:* MB, NN, ViU.

C 27   THOUGHTS ON THEOLOGY
         1872

Only printing (1872): [all within a double-rule frame] GLEANINGS /
FROM / THEODORE PARKER'S WORKS, / WITH ADDITIONS. / THOUGHTS ON
THEOLOGY. / SELECTED, PREPARED AND PUBLISHED / BY / ROSS WINANS. /
[rule] / BALTIMORE: / JOHN P. DES FORGES. / 1872.

17pp. Cover title. *Locations:* MB, NN.

C 28   PRIMITIVE CHRISTIANITY
         1872

Only printing (1872): [all within a double-rule frame] GLEANINGS /
FROM / THEODORE PARKER'S WORKS, / WITH ADDITIONS. / [rule] /
PRIMITIVE CHRISTIANITY. / [rule] / SELECTED, PREPARED AND
PUBLISHED / BY / ROSS WINANS. / [rule] / BALTIMORE: / JOHN P. DES
FORGES. / 1872.

13pp. Cover title. *Locations:* MB, ViU.

C 29-C 34   FRATERNITY TRACTS
              [1881]
The order of numbers is arbitrary.

C 29   NATURAL RELIGION
         [1881]

Only printing [1881]: FRATERNITY TRACTS. / No. 1. / SELECTED FROM
THE WRITINGS OF THEODORE PARKER. / [rule] / NATURAL RELIGION. /
[rule] / [30 lines of text]

4pp. Head title. Published by The Fraternity, Boston. *Fraternity
Tracts,* no. 1. *Locations:* MB, MH.

C 30   ERRORS OF THE POPULAR THEOLOGY
         [1881]

Only printing [1881]: FRATERNITY TRACTS. / No. 2. / SELECTED FROM
THE WRITINGS OF THEODORE PARKER. / ERRORS OF THE POPULAR THEOLOGY. /
[rule] / [31 lines of text]

4pp. Head title. Published by The Fraternity, Boston. *Fraternity
Tracts,* no. 2. *Location:* MB.

C 31   MAN NATURALLY LOVES GOD
         [1881]

184

Only printing [1881]: FRATERNITY TRACTS. / No. 3. / SELECTED FROM
THE WRITINGS OF THEODORE PARKER. / MAN NATURALLY LOVES GOD. /
[rule] / [32 lines of text]

4pp. Head title. Published by The Fraternity, Boston. *Fraternity
Tracts,* no. 3. *Location:* MB.

C 32   THREE MISTAKES OF THE CHRISTIAN CHURCH
[1881]

Only printing [1881]: FRATERNITY TRACTS. / No. 4. / SELECTED FROM
THE WRITINGS OF THEODORE PARKER. / THREE MISTAKES OF THE CHRISTIAN
CHURCH. / [rule] / [31 lines of text]

4pp. Head title. Published by The Fraternity, Boston. *Fraternity
Tracts,* no. 4. *Locations:* MB, MH.

C 33   IDEAS OF GOD IN THE BIBLE
[1881]

Only printing [1881]: FRATERNITY TRACTS. / No. 5. / SELECTED FROM
THE WRITINGS OF THEODORE PARKER. / IDEAS OF GOD IN THE BIBLE. /
[rule] / [30 lines of text]

4pp. Head title. Published by The Fraternity, Boston. *Fraternity
Tracts,* no. 5. *Location:* MB.

C 34   RACHEL; OR THE CONSOLING POWER OF RELIGION
[1881]

Only printing [1881]: FRATERNITY TRACTS. / No. 6. / SELECTED FROM
THE WRITINGS OF THEODORE PARKER. / RACHEL; OR THE CONSOLING POWER
OF RELIGION. / [rule] / [29 lines of text]

4pp. Head title. Published by The Fraternity, Boston. *Fraternity
Tracts,* no. 6. *Location:* MB.

C 35   THEODORE PARKER. PASSAGES FROM HIS WRITINGS
        [1885]

Fifth printing [1885]: FREEDOM, FELLOWSHIP AND CHARACTER IN
RELIGION. / Unity Mission / No. 19. / Single copies, 5 cts.; 10
copies, 25 cts. / UNITY OFFICE, 175 DEARBORN STREET, CHICAGO. /
THEODORE PARKER. / [rule] / PASSAGES FROM HIS WRITINGS, SELECTED BY
ALBERT WALKLEY. / [rule] / THEODORE PARKER: A SKETCH . . . PAGE.
[immediately over] 1 / TRUTH AGAINST THE WORLD: *a Parable of Paul*
2 / [eight lines of contents in double-columns] / [rule] / THEODORE
PARKER: A Sketch. / [21 lines of text in double-columns]

14pp. Head title. *Unity Mission*, no. 19. Price, 5¢. *Location:*
RPB (5th thousand).

Note: No copies earlier than the fifth thousand have been located.

Sixth printing [1885]: The title page is the same as in the fifth
printing.

14pp. Head title. *Unity Mission*, no. 19. Price, 5¢. *Location:*
MH-AH (6th thousand).

C 36   VIEWS OF RELIGION
        1885

First printing (1885): VIEWS OF RELIGION. / BY / THEODORE PARKER. /
[gothic] With an Introduction, / BY JAMES FREEMAN CLARKE. / [rule] /
BOSTON: / AMERICAN UNITARIAN ASSOCIATION. / 1885.

466pp. Deposit copy: BL (14 June 1886). Price, $1.00. *Locations:*
BL, JM, MH-AH, ViU.

Contents and printing histories: selections from *A Discourse of
Matters Pertaining to Religion*, see A 3; *Sermons of Theism, Atheism,
and the Popular Theology*, see A 36; *Ten Sermons of Religion*, see
A 32; *Lessons from the World of Matter and the World of Man*, see

A 64; *Discourses of Theology*, see C 6; and reprints of "The Relation
of Jesus to His Age and the Ages," see A 8; "A Discourse on the
Transient and Permanent in Christianity," see A 2; "A Sermon of
Immortal Life," see A 14; "An Humble Tribute to the Memory of
William Ellery Channing," see A 4.

Second printing (1888): The title page is the same as in the first
printing, except: 'VIEWS . . . CLARKE. / SECOND EDITION. / BOSTON:
. . . ASSOCIATION. / 1888.'.

466pp. *Location:* MH.

Third printing (1890): The title page is the same as in the first
printing, except: 'VIEWS . . . CLARKE. / THIRD EDITION. / BOSTON:
. . . ASSOCIATION. / 1890.'.

466pp. MH-AH copy received 25 June 1890. *Locations:* JM, MH-AH.

Fourth printing (1894): The title page is the same as in the first
printing, except: 'VIEWS . . . CLARKE. / FOURTH EDITION. / BOSTON:
. . . ASSOCIATION. / 1894.'.

466pp. *Location:* CtY.

Fifth printing (1900): The title page is the same as in the first
printing, except: 'VIEWS . . . CLARKE. / FIFTH EDITION. / BOSTON:
. . . ASSOCIATION. / 1900.'.

466pp. *Location:* JM.

Sixth printing (1906): VIEWS OF RELIGION / BY / THEODORE PARKER /
[gothic] With an Introduction / BY JAMES FREEMAN CLARKE / BOSTON /
AMERICAN UNITARIAN ASSOCIATION / 1906

466pp. *Locations:* MH-AH, ScU.

C 37   THE CHARACTER OF WASHINGTON
        [1887]

Only printing [1887]: [gothic] Old South Leaflets. / WASHINGTON'S
BIRTHDAY, 1887. / [rule] / The Character of Washington. / [rule] /
BY THEODORE PARKER.[1] / [rule] / [30 lines of text] / [1]Abridged from
the lecture in "Historic Americans."

8pp. Head title. Published by the Directors of the Old South
Work, Boston. Reprinted from *Historic Americans*, see A 65. *Old
South Leaflets*   *Location:* MH.

C 38   THE WORLD OF MATTER AND THE SPIRIT OF MAN
        [1907]

Only printing [1907]: THE WORLD OF MATTER / AND / THE SPIRIT OF
MAN / LATEST DISCOURSES OF RELIGION / BY / THEODORE PARKER / EDITED
WITH NOTES / BY / GEORGE WILLIS COOKE / [publisher's logo] /
BOSTON / AMERICAN UNITARIAN ASSOCIATION / 25 BEACON STREET

428pp. *Centenary Edition*, vol. [6] (see B 3). Copyright, 25
November 1907. MH-AH copy received 14 January 1908. Price, $1.00.
Locations: InU, JM, MBAt, MH, MH-AH, NcU.

Contents and printing histories: "Transcendentalism," see A 66;
"Ecclesiastical Institutions and Religious Consciousness," see C 6;
"The Biblical, Ecclesiastical, and Philosophical Notion of God,"
see A 55; "The Delights of Piety," see C 6; "Beauty in the World of
Matter," see A 57; "God's Revelation in Matter and Mind," first
printing (from Rufus Leighton's notes); "Theological and
Philosophical Development of New England," first printing (from
Parker's manuscript).

C 39   THE AMERICAN SCHOLAR
        [1907]

Only printing [1907]: THE AMERICAN SCHOLAR / BY / THEODORE PARKER /

EDITED WITH NOTES / BY / GEORGE WILLIS COOKE / [publisher's logo] /
BOSTON / AMERICAN UNITARIAN ASSOCIATION / 25 BEACON STREET

534pp. *Centenary Edition*, vol. [8] (see B 3). Copyright, 25
November 1907. MBAt copy received 26 November 1907. MH-AH copy
received 14 January 1908. Price, $1.00. *Locations:* JM, MBAt, MH,
MH-AH, NcU.

Contents and printing histories: "The American Scholar," see A 29;
"Ralph Waldo Emerson," see C 12; "William Ellery Channing," see
C 12; "Prescott as an Historian," see C 12; "Prescott's Conquest of
Mexico," see C 12; "Hildreth's United States," see C 12; "Macaulay's
History of England," *Massachusetts Quarterly Review*, 2 (June 1849):
326-355; "Buckle's History of Civilization," see C 13; "Henry Ward
Beecher," *Atlantic*, 1 (May 1858): 862-870; "Life and Character of
Dr. Follen," *Dial*, 3 (January 1843): 343-362; "German Literature,"
see A 6.

C 40 THE TRANSIENT AND PERMANENT IN CHRISTIANITY [1908]

Only printing [1908]: THE / TRANSIENT AND PERMANENT / IN
CHRISTIANITY / BY / THEODORE PARKER / EDITED WITH NOTES / BY /
GEORGE WILLIS COOKE / [publisher's logo] / BOSTON / AMERICAN
UNITARIAN ASSOCIATION / 25 BEACON STREET

482pp. *Centenary Edition*, vol. [4] (see B 3). Copyright, 21
August 1908. MH-AH copy received 24 December 1908. Price, $1.00.
Locations: InU, JM, MBAt, MH, MH-AH, NcU.

Contents and printing histories: "The Transient and Permanent in
Christianity," see A 2; "The Relation of Jesus to His Age," see
A 8; "The Relation of the Bible to the Soul," *Western Messenger*,
8 (December 1840, January 1841): 337-340, 389-396; "The
Christianity of Christ, of the Church, and of Society," see A 6;
"The Pharisees," see A 6; "Primitive Christianity," see A 6;

"Thoughts on Theology," see A 6; "The Excellence of Goodness," see A 9; "The Christian Use of Sunday," see A 18; "The Personality of Jesus," see C 12; "The Function of a Teacher of Religion," see A 46; "False and True Theology," see A 51; "A False and True Revival of Religion," see A 52; "The Revival [of Religion Which] We Need," see A 53; "A Bumblebee's Thoughts," see C 13.

C 41   SERMONS OF RELIGION
[1908]

Only printing [1908]: SERMONS OF RELIGION / BY / THEODORE PARKER / EDITED WITH A PREFACE / BY / SAMUEL A. ELIOT / [publisher's logo] / BOSTON / AMERICAN UNITARIAN ASSOCIATION / 25 BEACON STREET

346pp. *Centenary Edition,* vol. [3] (see B 3). Copyright, 6 January 1909. MH-AH copy received 24 December 1908. Price, $1.00. *Locations:* InU, JM, MBAt, MH, MH-AH, NcU.

Contents and printing histories: Ten Sermons of Religion, see A 32; "Of Religious Rest," unlocated; "Of Immortal Life," see A 14.

C 42   SINS AND SAFEGUARDS OF SOCIETY
[1909]

Only printing [1909]: SINS AND SAFEGUARDS OF / SOCIETY / BY / THEODORE PARKER / EDITED WITH NOTES / BY / SAMUEL B. STEWART / [publisher's logo] / BOSTON / AMERICAN UNITARIAN ASSOCIATION / 25 BEACON STREET

388pp. *Centenary Edition,* vol. [9] (see B 3). MH-AH copy received 7 March 1910. Price, $1.00. *Locations:* InU, JM, MBAt, MH, MH-AH, NcU.

Contents and printing histories: "The Chief Sins of the People," see A 26; "The Three Chief Safeguards of Society," see A 28; "The Public Education of the People," see A 22; "Education of the People," see A 22; "The Public Function of Woman," see A 34; "Home

Considered in Relation to Its Moral Influence," first printing (from Parker's manuscript); "The Moral Dangers of Prosperity," see A 43; "Hard Times," *Boston Daily Bee*, 5 October 1857; "Poverty," see A 29; "War," see A 12; "Crime and Its Punishment," first printing (from Parker's manuscript); "What Religion May Do For a Man," see A 59.

C 43   SOCIAL CLASSES IN A REPUBLIC
[1910]

Only printing [1910]: SOCIAL CLASSES IN A / REPUBLIC / BY / THEODORE PARKER / EDITED WITH NOTES / BY / SAMUEL A. ELIOT / [publisher's logo] / BOSTON / AMERICAN UNITARIAN ASSOCIATION / 25 BEACON STREET

346pp. *Centenary Edition*, vol. [10] (see B 3). MH-AH copy received 7 March 1910. Price, $1.00. *Locations:* InU, JM, MBAt, MH, MH-AH, NcU.

Contents and printing histories: "The Mercantile Classes," see A 15; "The Laboring Classes," see A 6; "The Education of the Laboring Classes," see A 3; "The Perishing Classes," see A 13; "The Dangerous Classes," see A 16; "The Aged," see A 37; "Material Conditions," see A 62; "Moral Conditions," see A 21; "Spiritual Conditions," see A 21.

C 44   THE SLAVE POWER
[1910]

First printing [1910]: THE SLAVE POWER / BY / THEODORE PARKER / EDITED WITH NOTES / BY / JAMES K. HOSMER / [publisher's logo] / BOSTON / AMERICAN UNITARIAN ASSOCIATION / 25 BEACON STREET

406pp. *Centenary Edition*, vol. [11] (see B 3). MH-AH copy received 26 May 1910. Price, $1.00. *Locations:* InU, JM, MBAt, MH, MH-AH, NcU.

Contents and printing histories: "A Sermon of Slavery," see A 7; "The Mexican War," see A 20; "A Letter of Slavery," see A 17; "The

Destination of America," see A 29; "The Abolition of Slavery by the French Republic," see A 29; "The Anti-Slavery Convention," see A 29; "The Free Soil Movement," see A 29; "Reply to Webster," see A 23; "The Slave Power," see A 29; "The Function of Conscience," see A 24; "The Boston Kidnapping," see A 30.

Second printing (1969): New York: Arno Press, 1969. Deposit copy: DLC (20 July 1970). Price, $14.50. *Locations:* DLC, ScU.

C 45   THE RIGHTS OF MAN IN AMERICA
[1911]

First printing [1911]: THE RIGHTS OF MAN / IN AMERICA / BY / THEODORE PARKER / EDITED WITH A PREFACE / BY / F. B. SANBORN / [publisher's logo] / BOSTON / AMERICAN UNITARIAN ASSOCIATION / 25 BEACON STREET

490pp. *Centenary Edition,* vol. [12] (see B 3). Copyright, 26 May 1911. MH-AH copy received 25 May 1911. Price, $1.00. *Locations:* InU, JM, MBAt, MH, MH-AH, NcU.

Contents and printing histories: "The Mexican War," see A 20; "The Administration of President Polk," see C 12; "The State of the Nation," see A 25; "The Life and the Different," see C 13; "The Fugitive Slave Law," see A 45; "An Anti-Slavery Address," see A 39; "The Progress of America," see A 45; "The New Crime Against Humanity," see A 40; "The Rights of Man in America," see A 42; "The Present Aspect of the Anti-Slavery Enterprise," see A 48; "The Present Crisis in American Affairs," see A 48.

Second printing [1969]: New York: Negro Universities Press, [1969]. Deposit copy: DLC (4 February 1970). Price, $12.00. *Locations:* DLC, ScU.

C 46   AUTOBIOGRAPHY, POEMS, AND PRAYERS
        [1911?]

Only printing [1911?]: AUTOBIOGRAPHY, POEMS / AND PRAYERS / BY /
THEODORE PARKER / EDITED WITH NOTES / BY / RUFUS LEIGHTON /
[publisher's logo] / BOSTON / AMERICAN UNITARIAN ASSOCIATION / 25
BEACON STREET

486pp. *Centenary Edition*, vol. [13] (see B 3). Price, $1.00.
Locations: InU, JM, MBAt, MH, NcU.

Contents and printing histories: "An Autobiographical Fragment,"
see *Life and Correspondence* (C 5); "The True Idea of a Christian
Church," see A 11; "Some Account of My Ministry," see A 33; "On the
Position and Duty of a Minister," see A 33; *Prayers,* see A 63;
"Truth Against the World," see A 6; "How to Move the World," see
A 6; "Parable of Ishmael," "A Parable," *Liberty Bell* (Boston:
Massachusetts Anti-Slavery Fair, 1846), pp. 21-24; "Parable of
Nathan Ben Elim," unlocated; *Theodore Parker's Experience as a
Minister,* see A 58; "Evening," Alfred P. Putnam, *Singers and Songs
of a Liberal Faith* (Boston: Roberts Brothers, 1875), p. 297; "The
Pilgrim's Star," Charles H. Crandall, *Representative Sonnets by
American Poets* (Boston: Houghton, Mifflin, 1891), p. 251; "To ——,"
see *Life and Correspondence* (C 5), 1:289-290; "Guidance," Octavius
Brooks Frothingham, *Theodore Parker* (New York: Putnam's, 1874), p.
507; "Golden Wedding. Samuel May and His Wife," see *Life and
Correspondence* (C 5), 2:28-29; "Jesus" ["Jesus, there is . . ."],
see C 12; "The Gospel of Love," Frothingham, *Theodore Parker*, p.
331; "Trials," Frothingham, *Theodore Parker*, p. 520; "Aspiration,"
Frothingham, *Theodore Parker*, pp. 374-375; "Evening Hymn,"
Frothingham, *Theodore Parker*, pp. 59-60; "To an Unknown Lover Who
Sent Flowers," Frothingham, *Theodore Parker*, pp. 243-244; "Jesus"
["Oh, thou . . ."], see C 12; "Human Misery, Heavenly Relief,"
unlocated; "The Good Shepherd," Frothingham, *Theodore Parker*, p.
536; "Ode to Commemorate the First Anniversary of the Surrender of
Thomas Simms," *First Anniversary—of the—Kidnapping of Thomas
Simms, April 12, 1852* (n.p.: n.p., 1852), broadside; "Webster.

1850," see "A Sonnet for the Times," C 12; "The Mission of Jesus," see "Dear Jesus . . .," C 12; "Almighty Love," see *Life and Correspondence* (C 5), 2:39; "Prayer," see *Life and Correspondence* (C 5), 2:30–40; "A Garden. From the German," unlocated; "Language of the Eyes. From the German of Rückert," see *Life and Correspondence* (C 5), 2:30; "The Sphinx. From the German of Heine," see *Life and Correspondence* (C 5), 2:31–32; "When We Were Children. From the German of Heine," "My Child When We Were Children. (From the German of Heine.)," *Gifts of Genius: A Miscellany of Prose and Poetry by American Authors* (New York: C. A. Davenport, 1859), pp. 184–185; "The Little Flower. From the German of Heine," *Life and Correspondence* (C 5), 2:35; "Mohnike, in Wilhelmi's Lyrick," "Two Lovers. (From the German of Mohnike.)," *Gifts of Genius*, pp. 181–183; "Fragment from Geibel's 'Tannhauser,'" *Life and Correspondence* (C 5), 2:36–37; "My Darling. From the German of Heine," *Life and Correspondence* (C 5), 2:34; "The Wanderer. From the German of Heine," *Life and Correspondence* (C 5), 2:35; "From the Russian," *Life and Correspondence* (C 5), 2:34; "The Farewell. From the German of Heine," *Life and Correspondence* (C 5), 2:35; "From Martin Opitz," *Life and Correspondence* (C 5), 2:37–38; "Hymn No. 1400 in Chevelier Bunsen's Collection," *Life and Correspondence* (C 5), 2:38.

C 47   SAINT BERNARD AND OTHER PAPERS
[1911]

Only printing [1911]: SAINT BERNARD / AND OTHER PAPERS / BY / THEODORE PARKER / EDITED WITH NOTES / BY / CHARLES W. WENDTE / [publisher's logo] / BOSTON / AMERICAN UNITARIAN ASSOCIATION / 25 BEACON STREET

483pp. *Centenary Edition*, vol. [14] (see B 3). Copyright, 15 December 1911. MH–AH copy received 16 December 1911. Price, $1.00. *Locations:* InU, JM, MBAt, MH, MH–AH, NcU.

Contents and printing histories: "The Life of Saint Bernard of Clairvaux," see A 6; "Cudworth's Intellectual System," *Christian*

Examiner, 27 (January 1840): 289–319; "A Letter to the Boston
Association of Congregational Ministers," see A 10; "A Friendly
Letter to the Executive Committee," see A 35; "The Law of God and
the Statutes of Men," see A 41; "The Consequences of an Immoral
Principle and False Idea of Life," see A 44; *The Two Christmas
Celebrations*, see A 60; "Theodore Parker to a Young Man," see A 67;
"A Letter Concerning a Plan of Reading," reprinted from the
Christian Register; "A New Lesson for the Day," see A 49; "The
Aspect of Slavery in America," see A 50; "The Effect of Slavery
Upon the American People," see A 56; "Parker's Indictment, and the
Fugitive Slave Cases," selections from *The Trial of Theodore Parker*,
see A 47; "Parker and the John Brown Campaign," various selections
by F. B. Sanborn.

C 48   THEODORE PARKER: AN ANTHOLOGY
        [1960]

Only printing [1960]: [flush left] THEODORE PARKER: / [flush right]
An Anthology / [two lines flush left] *Edited, with an Introduction
and Notes, by* / HENRY STEELE COMMAGER / Beacon Press   [publisher's
logo] Boston

391pp. Dust jacket. Copyright, 13 October 1960. Price, $6.00.
Locations: InU, JM.

C 49   QUOTATIONS ON LIBERAL RELIGION
        [1960]

Only printing [1960]: theodore parker / QUOTATIONS ON LIBERAL
RELIGION / ADVICE TO MINISTERS / Compiled by James H. Curtis /
Proposed by the Parker Memorial Committee / The American Unitarian
Association / 25 Beacon Street, Boston 8 / RELEASED IN HONOR OF THE
THEODORE PARKER CENTENNIAL YEAR 1860–1960

4pp. (printed on rectos only). Mimeographed. Cover title.
Location: MH–AH.

C 50   THE ASPIRATIONS OF THEODORE PARKER
         [1960]

Only printing [1960]: THEODORE PARKER / CENTENNIAL / [flag design] /
THE ASPIRATIONS / *of Theodore Parker* / EDITED BY / REV. GRETA
WORSTELL / *Church of the Reconciliation, Utica, New York* / [flag
design] / THE THEODORE PARKER MEMORIAL COMMITTEE / 1860–1960 /
[eight lines listing the 15 members of the Committee]

15pp. Cover title. *Location:* MH–AH.

C 51   THEODORE PARKER: AMERICAN TRANSCENDENTALIST
         1973

Only printing (1973): THEODORE PARKER: / American
Transcendentalist / A Critical Essay and a Collection / of his
Writings / by / Robert E. Collins / [publisher's logo] / The
Scarecrow Press, Inc. / Metuchen, N.J.   1973

271pp. Copyright, 30 October 1973. Deposit copy: DLC (6 November
1973). Price, $7.50. *Locations:* DLC, JM.

Contents and printing histories: "Transcendentalism," see A 66; "A
Discourse on the Transient and Permanent in Christianity," see A 2;
"The American Scholar," see A 29; "Political Destiny of America,"
see A 29; "The Writings of Ralph Waldo Emerson," see C 12; "A
Sermon of War," see A 12.

C 52   [SELECTIONS]
         [N.D.]

Only printing [n.d.]: Great Leaders — Number Two. / U. S. S.
SOCIETY, 25 BEACON ST., BOSTON / [engraving of Parker within a
single-rule frame] / THEODORE PARKER.

Single sheet folded once to make four pages. *Great Leaders*, no. 2
Location: MH–AH.

SECTION D:
BOOKS EDITED BY PARKER

D 1   A CRITICAL AND HISTORICAL INTRODUCTION TO THE CANONICAL
       SCRIPTURES OF THE OLD TESTAMENT
       1843

First printing (1843): A / CRITICAL AND HISTORICAL / INTRODUCTION /
TO THE / CANONICAL SCRIPTURES / OF THE / OLD TESTAMENT. / [gothic]
From the German / OF / WILHELM MARTIN LEBERECHT DE WETTE. /
TRANSLATED AND ENLARGED / BY / THEODORE PARKER, / MINISTER OF THE
SECOND CHURCH IN ROXBURY. / [rule] / [one line in Greek] / [rule] /
IN TWO VOLUMES. / VOL. I. [II.] / [rule] / BOSTON: / CHARLES C.
LITTLE AND JAMES BROWN. / [rule] / 1843.

517pp., 570pp. Parker wrote a friend on 10 October 1842 that it
"is in the press, and about 300pp. of the first volume are
stereotyped," adding: "About the first of April, 1843, I think it
may see the light" (Weiss, *Life and Correspondence* [C 5], 1:188).
Deposited for copyright: title: 5 September 1843; book, 14 September
1843. Deposit copy: DLC (14 September 1843). Inscribed copy:
MH-AH (12 August 1844). Listed by John Chapman in his
advertisements as an importation at 1d8s the set. *Locations:* DLC,
InU, MH-AH.

Note: Parker wrote a friend on 6 March 1858 that "It cost me 2000
dollars to stereotype it; I have received about 775 dollars back
again!" (Weiss, *Life and Correspondence* [C 5], 1:366).

Second printing (1850): The title page is the same as in the first
printing, except: 'A . . . [II.] / SECOND EDITION. / BOSTON: . . .
[rule] / 1850.'.

517pp., 570pp. Listed in the *English Catalogue* as an importation
at 24s the set. *Location:* DLC.

Third printing (1858): The title page is the same as in the second
printing, except: 'A . . . EDITION. / BOSTON: / LITTLE, BROWN AND
COMPANY. / 1858.'.

517pp., 570pp. Price, $3.75 the set. *Location:* RPB.

Note: Parker wrote George Ripley on 19 November 1858 that he was sending him a copy of "the third edition" (Weiss, *Life and Correspondence* [C 5], 1:401).

Fourth printing (1859): The title page is the same as in the second printing, except: 'A . . . ROXBURY / [rule] . . . [II.] / THIRD EDITION. / BOSTON: / RUFUS LEIGHTON, JR. / 1859.'.

517pp., 570pp. MH–AH copy received 18 March 1860. Price $3.75 the set. *Locations:* MB, MH–AH.

SECTION E:
MISCELLANEOUS

E 1   TWO LECTURES ON THE PRESENT CRISIS
        [1860]

TWO LECTURES / ON / THE PRESENT CRISIS, / BY THE LATE / THEODORE
PARKER / AND THE LATE / HON. HENRY CLAY. / DELIVERED AT DODWORTH'S
HALL, ON THE MORNING AND EVENING / OF SUNDAY, DEC. 16, 1860. /
[rule] / MRS. C. L. V. HATCH, MEDIUM. / [rule] / [gothic] "They
being Dead yet Speak." / [rule] / [rule] / NEW YORK: / PUBLISHED
BY S. T. MUNSON, Agt. / 143 FULTON-STREET.

Wrappers. "Lecture by the Late Theodore Parker," pp. 5–23.
Location: RPB.

E 2   MARIGOLDS BY THE WAYSIDE
        1870

[See the illustration on p. 204.]

158pp. *Location:* JM.

E 3   FOOD FOR THE MILLION
        1875

FOOD FOR THE MILLION; / OR, / THOUGHTS FROM BEYOND THE BORDERS / OF
THE MATERIAL. / BY / THEODORE PARKER, / THROUGH THE HAND OF / SARAH
A. RAMSDELL, / MEDIUM. / [four lines of verse] / BOSTON: /
PUBLISHED FOR THE AUTHOR. / 1875.

156pp. *Location:* DLC.

E 4   SPIRIT LIFE OF THEODORE PARKER
        1876

SPIRIT LIFE / OF / THEODORE PARKER. / THROUGH THE INSPIRATION OF /
SARAH A. RAMSDELL. / [rule] / BOSTON: / PRESS OF RAND, AVERY, &
CO. / 1876.

Marigolds by the Wayside;

OR,

The Prose and Poetry of Life.

RENDERED BY

THEODORE PARKER,

THROUGH THE TRANCE CONDITION OF

SARAH A. RAMSDELL.

~~~~~

BOSTON:
ADAMS & COMPANY,
1870.

E 2

84pp. *Locations:* DLC, MH.

E 5   THE LESSONS OF THE AGES
1882

THE / LESSONS OF THE AGES, / BY THEODORE PARKER. / THROUGH THE
INSPIRATION OF / MISS S. A. RAMSDELL. / [four lines of verse] /
[rule] / BOSTON: / PUBLISHED FOR THE AUTHOR. / 43 KILBY STREET. /
1882.

175pp. *Location:* ScU.

E 6   SCIENCE MADE EASY
1882

SCIENCE MADE EASY. / BY / THEODORE PARKER, / THROUGH THE MEDIUMSHIP
OF / SARAH A. RAMSDELL. / [rule] / Thoughts are the sands in the
ocean of mindality, and / the world gathers them for the hope of
Heaven, and the / resurrection of Christ. / [rule] / The noon of
the nineteenth century gave light to the / world, and established a
system of communication between / Earth and Heaven. / [rule] /
PHILADELPHIA: / E. R. RAMSDELL, PUBLISHER. / 1882.

233pp. *Location:* CSt.

E 7   THEODORE PARKER   A SERIES OF LETTERS
1900

THEODORE PARKER / *A series of letters* / [rule] / BY / ALBERT
WALKLEY / [rule] / NEPONSET PRESS, BOSTON / 1900

127pp. "The letters, though children of the imagination, deal with
the facts in the life of Theodore Parker" (p. [iii]). *Locations:*
JM, MB.

INDEX

INDEX

Crosby, Nichols, & Company, A 30.1.a, A 32.1.a, A 33.1.

"The Crucifixion," A 68.

C. S. Francis & Company, A 29.1, A 30.1.a.

Cudworth, Ralph C., C 47.

"Cudworth's Intellectual System," C 47.

Curtis Butts, A 34.2.

Curtis, George William, A 14.3.c.

Curtis, James H., C 49.

Da Capo Press, C 5.

"The Dangerous Classes." *See A Sermon of the Dangerous Classes in Society.*

The Dangers from Slavery, A 42.2.

"The Dangers Which Threaten the Rights of Man in America." *See A Sermon of the Dangers Which Threaten the Rights of Man in America.*

Daniel Webster; His Life, Acts, and Death. Being An Address Delivered at the Melodeon, Boston, Massachusetts, on Sunday Morning, Oct. 31, 1852, A 31.4.

D. Appleton & Co., A 4.6.b, A 6.3.c, A 29.2.b, A 32.1.d, A 36.3.c, A 45.1.c, A 47.1.a$_2$, B 2, C 5.

"Dear Jesus Were Thy Spirit Now on Earth," C 12, C 46. *See also* "The Mission of Jesus."

"The Delights of Piety." *See* "On the Delights of Piety."

Desor, E., C 13.

"The Destination of America." *See* "The Political Destination of America."

De Wette, Wilhelm Martin Leberecht, D 1.

Dial, A 6.1, C 39.

Directors of the Old South Work, A 42.2, C 37.

A Discourse Occasioned by the Death of Daniel Webster, Preached at the Melodeon on Sunday, October 31, 1852, A 31.2, A 45, A 65.3, C 13.

A Discourse Occasioned by the Death of John Quincy Adams: Delivered at the Melodeon in Boston, March 5, 1848, A 19, A 29, A 65.3, C 7.

"A Discourse Occasioned by the Death of the Late President Taylor, Preached at the Melodeon, on Sunday, July 14, 1850," A 29, C 7.

A Discourse of Matters Pertaining to Religion, A 4, B 1–B 3, C 1, C 2, C 4, C 36.

A Discourse of the Function of a Teacher of Religion in These Times, Preached at the Ordination of Marshall [sic] G. Kimball, as Minister of the Free Church at Barre, Worcester County, Mass., on Wednesday, June 13, 1855, A 46, C 6, C 8, C 40.

"A Discourse of the Relation Between the Ecclesiastical Instruction and the Religious Consciousness of the American People. Delivered at the Opening of the Progressive Friends' Meeting-House, at Longwood, Chester County, Pennsylvania, May 19, 1855," C 6, C 38.

A Discourse on the Transient and Permanent in Christianity; Preached at the Ordination of Mr. Charles C. Shackford, in the Hawes Place Church in Boston, May 19, 1841, A 2, A 6, C 11, C 36, C 40, C 51.

Discourses of Politics, B 2, C 7.

Discourses of Slavery, B 2, C 9.

Discourses of Social Science, B 2, C 10.

"Henry Ward Beecher," C 39.

Higginson, Thomas Wentworth, A 4.9, A 34.2, B 3.

Hildreth, Richard, C 12.

"Hildreth's History of the United States," C 12, C 39.

Historic Americans, A 65, B 1- B 3, C 37.

H. O. Houghton and Company, A 60, A 63.

Hollis Street Council, A 10.

Holmes, John Hayne, A 2.5.

"Home Considered in Relation to Its Moral Influence," C 42.

Horace B. Fuller, A 4.6.c, A 6.3.d–e, A 14.3.c, A 29.2.c–d, A 36.3.d, A 45.1.a, A 45.1.d, A 47.1.a$_1$, A 65.1, B 2.

Hosmer, James K., B 3, C 44.

Houghton, Mifflin, C 46.

"How to Move the World," A 6, C 12, C 46.

"Human Institutions and National Life," A 64.

"Human Misery, Heavenly Relief," C 46.

"Human Progress," A 64.

An Humble Tribute to the Memory of William Ellery Channing, D.D. A Sermon Preached at West Roxbury, October 9th, 1842, A 5, C 36.

H. W. Swett & Co., A 57, A 59.

"Hymn No. 1400 in Chevelier Bunsen's Collection," C 46.

The Idea of a Christian Church. A Discourse at the Installation of Theodore Parker as Minister of the Twenty-Eighth Congregational Church in Boston, January 4, 1846, A 11, A 29, C 6, C 8, C 46.

Ideas of God in the Bible, C 33.

Immortality is a Fact of Man's Nature, C 23.

"The Influence of Religion Upon the Feelings," A 68.

The Influence of the Religious Element in Life, C 21.

I. R. Butts, A 11–A 13.

Jackson, Francis, A 61.

James Campbell, A 63.1.e, A 64.1.c.

James M'Callum, A 31.5.a.

James Munroe and Company, A 6.1, A 17.1.a.

J. B. Yerrinton and Son, A 34.1.

Jefferson, Thomas, A 65.

Jerome, A 4.1.a–c, A 4.2–9.

"Jesus" ["Jesus, there is . . ."], C 12, C 46.

"Jesus" ["Oh, thou . . ."], C 12, C 46.

"Jesus of Nazareth," A 64.

"Jesus There is No Name So Dear as Thine," C 12, C 46. *See also* "Jesus" ["Jesus, there is . . ."].

J. Maclehose, A 18.2.

"John Adams," A 65.

John Brown's Expedition Reviewed in a Letter from Rev. Theodore Parker, at Rome, to Francis Jackson, Boston, A 61, C 13.

John Chapman, A 4.1.c, A 4.2, A 4.5, A 6.2, A 32.2, A 34.3, A 36.2, A 55, A 58.3, D 1.

John Childs and Son, A 64.2.a, A 65.2, B 1.

John Edward Taylor, A 58.2.

John F. Trow, A 55, C 6.

John Green, A 5.2, A 6.1.

John P. Des Forges, C 14–C 28.

224